William J Fay 13 15 2041

Mark
The Gospel as Story

First published in Great Britain, 1983 by
T. & T. Clark Limited, 36 George Street,
Edinburgh EH2 2LQ.

ISBN: 0 567 09342 5

Phototypeset by
J. Swain & Son Ltd., Glasgow.

Printed by
Billing and Sons Ltd., Worcester.

Studies of the New Testament and its world

EDITED BY JOHN RICHES

Mark
The Gospel as Story

by

ERNEST BEST

T. & T. CLARK
36 GEORGE STREET
EDINBURGH

Contents

Preface

Lecturing on the Gospel of Mark is an occupational hazard for those who teach New Testament since it normally features in even the shortest course. Yet as those of us who teach rush to explain it so that we can get on to our own interests we often ignore certain basic questions. It is these questions which I have tried to identify, if not to answer. They relate to the nature of the Gospel, to the occasion of its composition, to what Mark was trying to achieve in writing it, to the nature of the contribution he made to the existing traditions about Jesus, and above all to what it is that holds it together so that it is clearly recognizable as a unity and not just as a collection of anecdotes.

This book is not then strictly a survey of other writing on Mark. Such surveys may be found in the studies of R.P. Martin, *Mark-Evangelist and Theologian* (see note 39) and H. Baarlink, *Anfängliches Evangelium* (see note 26), and more briefly in H.C. Kee, 'Mark's Gospel in Recent Research' in *Int* 32 (1978) 353–368. I have perforce covered some of the same ground as they, and of course some more recent work, not primarily in order to evaluate the contributions of others but for the light they have thrown on my own concerns and because they have opened up new ways of regarding the basic issues I have outlined above. What I present here is much more a personal reaction to the problems the Gospel raises, though in the notes I have tried to give as many references to others as possible. There are however not many references to the standard commentaries, like those of Taylor, Cranfield, Lohmeyer and Haenchen. In teaching Mark their work has been so incorporated into my thinking that my debt to them, even if it is by way of disagreement, must be everywhere evident. On the whole however they did not directly tackle the kind of questions in which I have been interested.

The genesis of this book was an invitation to deliver the Nils W. Lund Memorial Lectures at North Park Theological Seminary, Chicago in 1978, and I would again thank The Dean and Faculty for the invitation. Other portions were used in various places and in various forms. A great part of the material was used in a postgraduate seminar in Glasgow to whose members, in particular my colleague John K. Riches, I am indebted for many acute comments. I also thank the editors of *Irish Biblical Studies* and the *Proceedings of the Irish Biblical Association* for permission to reproduce material, though in an amended form, which they have published.

I would again thank my wife who toiled to type a very much written over manuscript and reduce it to the more or less legible form in which it now appears.

CHAPTER I

HISTORICAL SURVEY

Mark was a neglected Gospel until the nineteenth century. During that century there was a complete turn round and by its end the shortest Gospel was receiving the greatest attention. This came about through the rise in interest in the life of the historical Jesus. When scholars first began to attempt to write a life of Jesus they gave more or less equal authority to the different Gospels and indeed some considered John to be the most important. As discussion continued the synoptic problem was formulated and solved, at least temporarily, with the hypothesis of the priority of Mark. At the same time John was increasingly classed as theological interpretation containing little or no material of interest to the historian. In so far as any historical account of the life of Jesus could be given it was assumed that the order of events was roughly that of Mark's Gospel: a Galilean spring when the crowds accepted him, Caesarea Philippi as the turning point, the resolution to go to Jerusalem, rejection and the hero's death on the cross. To put this another way, the incidents in Mark are held together as sequential events in the life of Jesus; the inner structure of the Gospel is dependent on the historical order of events in Jesus' life.

Wrede[1] upset all this. Mark was much more theological and much less historical than had been assumed. Wrede, in common with many other scholars of the late nineteenth century, began with the assumption that Jesus had never thought of himself as messiah or son of God; yet the early church recognised his messianic nature. Why was it that the disciples had failed to recognise his true nature while they were with him? The Gospel was written as an attempt to explain this riddle, and it did so through among other things the commands to secrecy to the demons, the secret instruction of the disciples during Jesus' lifetime and their failure to understand him. The details of Wrede's particular theory were not as important as his discovery of theological tendencies within Mark.

Wrede's study was quickly followed by Schweitzer's *The Quest of the Historical Jesus* (or with the more literal translation of its

---

[1] W. Wrede, *Das Messiasgeheimnis in den Evangelien,* Göttingen, 1901.

German title 'From Reimarus to Wrede'[2]). Schweitzer argued that in searching for the historical Jesus nineteenth century scholars had closed their eyes to much of the evidence and so had not discovered the true Jesus but one whom they had carefully constructed out of their own presuppositions. Though it took quite a time to mature the consequence of the combined work of Wrede and Schweitzer was that many fewer lives of Jesus were written by major scholars (those of Goguel[3] and Bultmann[4] are outstanding exceptions) and these no longer looked to Mark as the backbone for their views of the historical Jesus.

If then Mark was no longer to be used mainly as a source of information about the historical Jesus to what use could the information it contained be turned? The form-critics quickly supplied an answer. The incidents in Mark's Gospel could be employed to tell us about the life of the early church. Thus the various incidents were categorised according to their form, set back into the life of the early church and seen in relation to its activities. With this there appeared a much more dynamic concept of the development of the Jesus-tradition. So far as the Gospel of Mark was concerned it meant that the Gospel framework was more or less dissolved. Interest no longer lay in the sequence of events, whether theologically or historically interpreted, but in the separate paragraphs divorced from one another.

But books cannot in the end be regarded merely as quarries for information about communities. Once they are written they have an existence of their own and we have to ask why they were written. So discussion on Mark has turned around once again and the Gospel is now viewed as a whole. In what lies its unity and how is that unity expressed? These are the kind of questions with which this book is concerned, but before we can take them up we must retrace our steps a little to look at one or two points in more detail so that we can more adequately understand the problem.

---

[2] A. Schweitzer, *Von Reimarus zu Wrede,* Tübingen, 1906.
[3] M. Goguel, *La Vie de Jésus,* Paris, 1932.
[4] R. Bultmann, *Jesus,* 1926.

CHAPTER II

THE PRE-MARKAN MATERIAL

As everyone knows the assumption of the priority of Mark and the existence of Q has been called in question within the last twenty years and serious inroads have been made on a simple literary solution to the synoptic problem. Solutions which suppose that Matthew and Luke were sources for Mark raise greater difficulties than they solve. A purely literary solution to the problem is in any case inadequate. When Mark wrote the incidents which he recorded were not wiped out of the minds of men because he had recorded them. They still continued to exist as oral or possibly written tradition. Matthew and Luke knew many of the incidents, not only in the form which they read in Mark's Gospel, but also in variant form in the oral tradition. As they wrote they made use of these variant forms as well as what they read in Mark. Thus in many cases they agree between themselves and disagree with Mark. Yet they had Mark before them and he supplied an order for the events, and this was natural since the oral tradition they possessed had no order. Thus when Matthew wrote he had not only before him the written Gospel of Mark and the material which came to him in Q, whether that was one source or a number of sources need not concern us, and the material of his special sources which are normally termed M, but he also had many of the incidents in Mark still alive in oral form; he would naturally substitute in the Markan outline the form known to his own community or would modify the Markan form to bring it into line with that form. Since in what follows we are not concerned with Matthew or Luke we do not need to trace this further, and we shall proceed from the assumption that Mark's Gospel was the first. The fact, however, that Matthew and Luke may have known the tradition which is contained in Mark in a variant form means that we may be able to learn a little bit about how Mark modified the tradition as he used it, though, of course, we cannot be sure in respect of any particular incident that Mark actually had it in the same form as Matthew or Luke received it when they came to write.

Turning now from source criticism we must look briefly at form criticism and what it means for our understanding of Mark. It is only necessary to draw attention to a few features. Stories which originally had a situation in the life of Jesus as they were handed on in the oral tradition came to have a situation within the life of the community. This situation was not static and the same incident might be used for different purposes. If we assume that Luke reflects the oral tradition of his community then the parable of the lost sheep was used in it to depict the love of God for the sinner; if Matthew reflects the oral tradition of his community then the same parable was used in it to show how a good pastor should look after the members of the community. The interpretation of the parable of the sower (Mk 4.14–20) shows how that parable came to be understood in the developing tradition once the original sense given to it by Jesus had been lost. Stories of Jesus were kept alive and repeated because they met the needs of the growing church. We can assume that the problem of the payment of taxes existed wherever Christians recognised the kingship of Jesus, and so his discussion about whether taxes should be paid to Caesar or not continued to guide the church. Missionaries were being sent out from established Christian communities into other areas and needed instructions for their work; the instructions given in Matthew (10.1ff.) and Mark (6.7–11) are not the same and the variations were probably caused by the different problems encountered by missionaries in different parts of Europe and Asia. The story of the Last Supper would be used in the church when worshipping in a Eucharistic service and probably the account of the feeding of the five thousand was moulded to fit the shape of the Eucharist. The church continued to be involved in controversy with the Jews and so accounts of Jesus' discussions with them would be of use (Mk 2.23–3.5; 7.1–23; Mt 23.1ff.). But not all the material used in the early church and recorded in our Gospels necessarily went back to Jesus himself. Some of it for various reasons may have come into existence after his death and then been attributed to him. The rules for church discipline (Mt 18.15–17) probably arose out of the need of the community to deal with difficult situations within itself. The instruction to baptise in the name of the Trinity (Mt 28.16–20) does not go back to Jesus. In summary there are three things to say: (i) The community discarded accounts of Jesus which seemed of no importance to itself; (ii) it preserved those which met its needs and modified them so that they were more appropriate; (iii) it created material, perhaps through the work of Christian prophets, which was then attributed to Jesus.[5]

The incidents were thus used for different purposes and as such they existed and were used in isolation from one another. There is

[5] Other insights given by form-criticism will appear as we go on.

nothing unusual in the preservation of oral material as discrete incidents. A.P. Lord comments that in the normal way in which they are told oral traditional narratives about individuals 'rarely include a single account that begins with birth and ends with death. Most commonly, separate elements or incidents in the life of the hero form individual poems or sagas'.[6] He illustrates this from the cycles of stories about Marko Kraljević and Cúchulainn. A particular church would know the parable of the sower, the account of the dispute about tax with the penny, the story of the Last Supper, but would not set them in relation to one another. Each was useful in its own sphere of concern. Perhaps some incidents were connected together because they were of a similar nature or related in some other way to one another. Thus there may have been a collection of parables (Mk 4.1–34) or a catena or sequence of miracle stories (Mk 4.35ff.), but they will have been put together not because they happened together within the life of Jesus, but because they were used to meet a common need within the church.[7]

When incidents circulate separately they quickly lose the data of time and space by which they were originally connected to one another. It makes little difference to the truth of the Golden Rule when or where Jesus spoke it or whether he spoke it on one or many occasions. So the parables, healings and sayings of Jesus would circulate without any specific mention of the day on which they happened and therefore in no chronological relation to one another. Similarly when the stories were being told in areas remote from Palestine to people who knew nothing about its geography it soon became irrelevant to give details of their locality. The names of people also disappeared from stories; it is of no importance to record the identity of those who are healed when they are unknown to the hearers of the story. It is then no surprise when we turn to the Gospel of Mark and find a great lack, though not a total absence of temporal, spatial and personal information. Incidents are regularly united to one another with the simple temporal statement 'and immediately'. It is difficult to make geographical sense of the journeys of Jesus across the Lake. Only in a few cases do we find the names of those who have been healed or of those who have interrogated Jesus. Further evidence of the unimportance of details of time, place and name can be seen when we compare the Gospels with one another. If the Gospels can vary

---

[6] A.B. Lord, 'The Gospels as Oral Traditional Literature', in *The Relationships among the Gospels* (ed. W.O. Walker), San Antonio, Texas, 1978, pp. 39f.

[7] For a recent discussion see H.W. Kuhn, *Ältere Sammlungen im Markusevangelium* (StUNT 8), Göttingen, 1971.

such details between themselves then it is highly probable that the earlier tradition varied or dropped details.[8] The scene is set differently in Mk 2.1f. and Mt 9.1; Mk 3.1 does not say on what Sabbath the incident of 3.2–5 took place; Mt 12.9 and Lk 6.6 give different solutions. Mk 3.23–30 is set in a different context in Mt 12.25–37 and Lk 11.17–23. In 9.51–18.14 Luke gives a long journey that is wholly lacking in Matthew and Mark; it is a deliberately constructed journey and much of the material from Q appearing in it does so in different contexts from its positioning in Matthew. Even the date of the death of Jesus was subject to variation within the early church; Mark and John set it in a different relation to the feast of the passover; it is as if in a close-knit family a son thought his mother died on Christmas day whereas a daughter thought she had died on Christmas eve!

The conclusion of all this is that the material as it existed in the oral tradition did not possess within itself an organisational principle, i.e., a principle by which the incidents could be set in relation to one another. This would still be true even if an outline account of the life of Jesus existed as Dodd suggested.[9] Whoever had to draw together the miracles, parables and sayings would still not have known where and how to relate them to one another. The preservation of such an outline is however improbable. If then the individual pericopae were to be put together how was this to be done? The form critics argued that the pericopae were preserved or created and preserved by the community; it is however only an individual who can provide and work out an organisational principle. Form critisism with its communal emphasis cannot therefore account for the appearance of the Gospels.[10]

---

[8] Cf. T. Boman, *Die Jesus-Überlieferung im Lichte der neueren Volkstunde*, Göttingen, 1967, pp. 1ff.

[9] C.H. Dodd, 'The Framework of the Gospel Narratives', in *New Testament Studies*, pp. 1–11, Manchester, 1953.

[10] E. Güttgemanns, *Candid Questions Concerning Form Criticism* (ET by W.G. Doty), Pittsburg, 1979, passim; see below for further discussion.

CHAPTER III

QUESTIONS

This brings us back to a question raised earlier, 'What is the unity which holds the Gospel together?' The original readers or hearers of the Gospel already knew all or almost all of the individual stories and sayings but knew them as discrete items. We can assume that Mark did not just put them together higgeldy-piggeldy for storage purposes and also that he did not intend what he wrote to be immediately divided up again. Down through the centuries preachers and teachers when they have used the Gospel have almost invariably done the latter, it being easier to use separate incidents as a basis for their preaching and teaching than the Gospel as a whole. But as Standaert[11] above all has continually emphasised the Gospel was intended to be read as a whole. Mark hoped it would achieve its effect through its total impact. Moreover he probably designed it to be heard rather than read. We today belong to a different educational system and our approach to literature is more often through the eye than the ear; this is especially so of academics who analyse literature. It is thus difficult for us to realise the importance of listening to the Gospel rather than reading it.

In addition to the question about the unity of the Gospel we can identify a number of related questions which require answers if we are to understand the Gospel. What organising principle or principles were used in putting the incidents together? If the original individual incidents each had its own *Sitz im Leben* within the community what is the *Sitz im Leben* of the whole Gospel? Why did Mark put the Gospel together? If the separate incidents can be classified under a limited number of forms can the Gospel itself be classified as a form which was known in the ancient world, or did Mark create a new form when he wrote his book? Why were the particular incidents selected that were selected and what intention lay behind the placing of them together? Where was the Gospel written? What was the occasion of its writing? That is to say, was there a particular event or succession of events which led Mark to put the Gospel together? Was there some outside cause other than

[11] B.H.M.G.M. Standaert, *L'Evangile selon Marc: composition et genre litteraire,* Nijmegen, 1978, pp. 3, 9, 26.

his own desire to produce a book? Why was it so long (forty years?) before the Gospel was written? For whom was it written, for the outside world as a weapon of evangelism or apologetic, or for the Christian community? What is the nature of Mark's authorship? Did those who first read it already know its content, at least as separate pericopae? From what we have said so far there seems little doubt that this final question must be answered in the affirmative; in what follows we shall therefore assume this answer; as we work through the material we shall find no reason to change it. What we have listed are a number of interdependent questions. The way in which we answer any particular one of them will determine how we answer most of the others. We may indeed not be able to answer any of them, or at least not with any certainty. But we have at least made an advance if we can identify the problems which require to be solved.

CHAPTER IV

THE REDACTION-CRITICAL APPROACH

Of course none of these questions can be answered without a knowledge of the content of the Gospel and so as we think them through we have also to think about the material which Mark has used and consider the ways in which he has used it. The content, its arrangement and its editing, are not just a matter of chance. If there has been an organising principle this will reveal itself in the way material has been put together and in the modifications which have been made to it. A redactor has been defined as 'one who senses the latent possibilities within a tradition'.[12] We require then to examine the content to see where and how the hand of Mark appears in its use. This brings us to the present stage of work on Mark, the stage of redaction criticism. This may not be the best label for this type of criticism, but it is the accepted one. As a deliberate method of study of the Gospels it appeared in the mid-fifties with the work of H. Conzelmann on Luke[13] and G. Bornkamm and his pupils on Matthew.[14] The first monograph on Mark was that of Willi Marxsen which he entitled significantly 'The Evangelist Mark'[15] and not 'The Gospel of Mark'. However the seeds of the Redaktionsgeschichtliche movement lay much further back in the work of Wrede[16] and probably also in that of Wellhausen.[17] Wrede's discussion of the messianic secret in the Gospel was an acknowledgement of Mark's own theology as a significant factor in what he wrote. The form critics had been well aware of the element of theology in the Gospel but since they were concerned with the material as it was used by the early church they eliminated

---

[12] L.H. Silberman, ' "Habent Sua Fata Libelli": The Role of Wandering Themes in Some Hellenistic Jewish and Rabbinical Literature', in W.O. Walker, *op. cit.* (as n. 6), p. 217.

[13] H. Conzelmann, *Die Mitte der Zeit,* Tübingen, 1954.

[14] G. Bornkamm, G. Barth, H.J. Held, *Überlieferung und Auslegung im Matthäusevangelium,* Neukirchen, 1960. This book contains Bornkamm's three essays which first made the redactional approach and were published in 1948, 1954 and 1956.

[15] W. Marxsen, *Der Evangelist Markus,* Göttingen, 1956 (ET; Nashville and New York, 1969). H. Riesenfeld's briefer study 'Tradition und Redaktion im Markusevangelium', in *Neutestamentliche Studien für R. Bultmann,* Berlin, 1954, moved along similar lines.

[16] Op. cit. (as n. 1).

[17] In his commentaries on Matthew (1904), Mark (1903) and Luke (1904). The idea may even be traced back to Reimarus, 'Von dem Zwecke Jesu und seiner Jünger' (1778), I, §§ 31, 32.

it in so far as they regarded it as Markan so that they could examine the individual pericopae without their Markan over-tones. What they eliminated became the centre of discussion for the redaction critics. Between the earlier work of the first form critics and the work of the redaction critics two scholars made important contributions: in England R.H. Lightfoot in two significant books, and again note their titles, 'History and Interpretation in the Gospels'[18] and 'Locality and Doctrine in the Gospels',[19] demonstrated how theology penetrated the whole of each Gospel; in Germany E. Lohmeyer, not only in his commentry on Mark,[20] but also in his other writings, showed the importance of the use of place names in Mark and in particular the importance attaching to the contrast between Galilee and Jerusalem.[21]

How do redaction critics go about their work? In the case of Matthew and Luke we can compare them one against the other in so far as they use material from Q and, more importantly, each against Mark in so far as they use him. We can note the modifications they make and look to see if these exhibit any consistency. If there is this will represent at least part of their view. In the case of Mark we have nothing with which we can compare his Gospel. The method of study is inevitably circular but as the work has proceeded certain important procedures have appeared. Redaction criticism depends upon the work of the form critics. The redaction critic accepts the material as the form critic says it appeared in the pre-Markan stage and enquires what changes Mark has made to it and asks how he has put it together. It is impossible to give here a systematic analysis of the methods used but we can point to one or two approaches which have proved important.

If the material lacked notes of time and place as it existed in the oral stage then the way in which Mark has united incidents to one another will reveal something of his work. Thus the first place to look is at the connecting seams by which Mark joins one pericope to another. These seams are examined for Markan linguistic characteristics: favourite words, e.g., *palin,* or idioms, e.g., *archomai* used as an auxiliary verb. We look secondly for Markan motifs or themes, e.g., the fear displayed by the disciples, their failure to understand (6.52). We find the same themes and language present in Markan summaries: 3.11f., where Mark says that the demons acknowledge Jesus as son of God and he tells them not

---

[18] London, 1935.
[19] London, 1938.
[20] Göttingen, 1937.
[21] *Galiläa und Jerusalem,* Göttingen, 1936.

to make him known, reflects what happens in the individual exorcisms. Naturally some Markan characteristics will appear within pericopae. When anyone retells a story they have heard from someone else they change certain words and idioms from those of the speaker to those which they themselves normally use. We may thus expect to find some Markan characteristics within the pericopae, but they will not occur as frequently or so closely together, as they do in the seams and summaries.[22] We should however beware of taking their presence within a pericope as evidence that Mark is creating material; he may only be retelling a story in his own words.

We do certainly find Mark at work within pericopae where he adds material. He frequently inserts clauses giving a brief explanation; these are introduced in Greek by the word *gar* ('for'): 1.16, 'for they were fishermen'; the Greek word for casting a net in the sea which precedes this clause is unusual and might not have been understood by Mark's Roman readers without the addition. A somewhat longer addition about the washing habits of Jews in respect of pots and pans is found in 7.3f; here most translations place Mark's explanation of the Jewish custom in brackets. In 11.14 he adds a brief clause 'for it was not the season for figs' in relation to Jesus' cursing of the fig tree and seems thereby to indicate that what happens is not intended to be taken literally but parabolically. He also appends brief concluding clauses to pericopae to give additional information; at the end of the prophecy of Peter's denial he adds after Peter's affirmation that he would not deny Jesus 'and they all said the same' (14.31); at the end of the account of the arrest he adds 'and they all forsook him, and fled' (14.50).

The third and most important piece of evidence to consider is the order in which Mark places his material; as I have constantly emphasised the material came to him without indication of the chronological order in which it should be placed. He often 'sandwiches' one event inside another so that the two throw light on each other: the cursing of the fig tree and the discovery of its withering sandwich the cleansing of the temple and indicate that the day of the temple is over. He created a journey for Jesus from Caesarea Philippi to Jerusalem in such a way that it is studded with predictions of his death and directed to instruction on discipleship.[23]

[22] See E.J. Pryke, *Redactional Style in the Marcan Gospel* (SNTS Monograph Series 33), Cambridge, 1978.

[23] See below, pp. 84ff.

We must be careful, however, not to suggest that Mark felt himself free to alter or create as he liked. There is no indication that he ever invented individual incidents; all the evidence goes to show that he used existing material adapting it to his purpose. There is positive evidence that he had a real respect for the tradition and preserved much of its detail faithfully.[24] Eusebius reports the tradition that Mark 'gave attention, to leave out nothing of what he had heard and to make no false statements in them'.[25] This however should not be taken to suggest that everything happened as Mark says it happened; the tradition almost certainly had been modified before it reached him; incidents may even have been invented in the early church; if they were we cannot hold Mark responsible. What we assert is his acceptance of the existing tradition in relation to the incidents which he records. We can see his respect for the tradition in the way in which he leaves detail unaltered when it would have suited his purpose to change it. In the first exorcism the demon confesses Jesus as 'the holy one of God' (1.24); elsewhere when the demons confess Jesus they confess him as 'son of God' and in 3.11f. where Mark himself is composing freely in order to summarise the activity of Jesus he makes them use this title. 'Son of God' has for Mark a special significance as a title of confession yet he has not altered 'the holy one of God' to 'son of God' even though the change would have been slight and easily made. In the three predictions of the death of Jesus (8.31; 9.31; 10.33f.) the resurrection is said to take place 'after three days'; the regular New Testament phrase is 'on the third day'. 'After three days' is not strictly correct; it implies at least 'on the fourth day'. Both Matthew and Luke change Mark at this point to bring the predictions into line with the normal phrase. Mark is using early tradition here and he has not harmonised it with the normal phrase and with the tradition he records in 16.1–8, possibly because his community knew the predictions (with 'after three days') in a liturgical or confessional context. In 10.29 Jesus makes a promise to those who have left house or brothers or sisters, or lands and this is made in relation to Peter who had not left lands but nets and fishing; Mark introduced Peter at this point as the spokesman of the disciples but he did not alter the traditional form of the saying. In 11.16 Jesus is said to forbid Jews from carrying

---

[24] For detailed discussion see Best, 'Mark's Preservation of the Tradition' in M. Sabbe, *L'Evangile selon Marc: Tradition et nédaction* (Gembloux, 1974), pp. 21–34 = 'Markus also Bewahrer der Überlieferung' in Das Markus-Evangelium (ed. R. Pesch; Darmstadt, 1979), pp. 390–409.

[25] *HE* III 39.15.

any vessel through the temple; this certainly fits into Jewish tradition but Mark makes no use of it in his narrative; he has preserved the detail because it was there. The 'titulus' on the cross is expressed as a Roman would express it 'the King of the Jews'[26]; it would have suited Mark much better if he had been able to replace this by 'the son of God' or 'the son of man'. Mark retains what lay in the tradition, though frequently (the confessions of the demons and the centurion, the testimony of the false witnesses at the trial) he likes to put on the lips of apparent opponents the truths about Jesus; a testimony of Pilate by means of the titulus to Jesus' sonship would have fitted well into this scheme. If, as many suppose, Jesus knew himself as the suffering servant, while Mark may accept this he does nothing to emphasise it[27]; it is not certain however that Jesus so knew himself. We need to recollect once again that Mark's readers already knew the stories he used; he could not therefore alter them radically and so he preserved their detail even though he might have preferred not to. Once he shows he is aware he is misusing a story, the cursing of the fig tree, when at 11.14 he inserts 'for it was not the time for figs'; the story must have been known to his readers as belonging to a period of the year when figs would be ripe. In his preservation of material Mark would be following the traditional role of the story-teller in at least some parts of the world. J.H. Delargy writes of 'the story-teller's realization of his responsibility as guardian of inherited tradition'.[28] Somewhat similarly A.B. Lord says that the picture which emerges (of the Slavic singer of tales) 'is not really one of conflict between preserver of tradition and creative artist; it is rather one of the preservation of tradition by the constant re-creation of it'.[29] Although Mark was transferring the oral material into a written form his responsibility to preserve tradition would still be there, though it might not exist beyond him.

If we say that Mark preserved the tradition this is not to imply that it was his primary intention in writing his book to preserve it; he was not an anthropologist with a tape recorder salvaging the ancient oral material for posterity. He had other purposes: in the course of carrying them out it was his practise to preserve the tradition as carefully as possible. People accustomed to oral tradition like to see it continue unchanged.

[26] Cf. H. Baarlink, *Anfängliches Evangelium: ein Beitrag zur näheren Bestimmung der theologischen Motive im Markusevangelium,* Kampen, 1977, pp. 287–8.

[27] Op. cit., pp. 238–242.

[28] 'The Gaelic Story-Teller. With some Notes on Gaelic Folk-Tales', *Proc. Brit. Acad.* 31(1945) 177–221, at p. 194.

[29] *The Singer of Tales,* London, 1960, p. 29.

Returning now to the simple fact that Mark put the material together we have seen that we cannot say much about his choice since we do not know what fund of material was at his disposal. He probably did not know the birth stories or the details of the temptation; we cannot then learn anything about his thinking from their omission. It is equally important not to try and learn too much from the details of stories he has included: that he uses the Parable of the Sower does not mean that his community consisted of farmers who would appreciate its every point; the command 'I will make you fishers of men' does not indicate that all his readers were fishermen. He used the material which was available to him in the tradition.

We do at least know the order in which he set the incidents he selected, that is to say, we know how he set them in relation to one another and that not merely to the incidents which directly precede and follow or to incidents of similar type but even the way in which he prepares for later incidents by earlier, the build up of material drawing out a common motif, the increasing stress on a particular theme, the gradual but steady approach to a partial or final conclusion. We wholly agree with Tannehill when he says 'Mark is a unified narrative because, in spite of clear division into episodes, there are connecting threads of purpose and development which bind the story together'.[30] As we have already indicated this is the most important aspect of the work of redaction critics – much more so than the analysis of connecting verses or the identification of Mark's hand within pericopae.

The way in which Mark worked must be distinguished from that of Matthew and Luke. As they wrote they had available at least one extensive document, Mark, and much other material; whether the latter was in oral or written form is more difficult to determine, as also whether it consisted of one or more documents or sets of material. In using Mark they 'improved' what he had written. If we speak of what they did as 'redaction' then we ought, perhaps, to speak of Mark's work as 'composition' and the way we deal with it as 'composition criticism' rather than 'redaction criticism'.

Since we have mentioned Matthew and Luke it is important to remind ourselves how necessary it is to forget them when reading Mark. We sub-consciously tend to amalgamate what we read in one Gospel with what we read in another; Matthew and Luke amplify Mark in many respects; we must be careful not to read their amplifications back into him. In 2.17 Jesus says according to

---

[30] R.C. Tannehill, 'The Gospel of Mark as Narrative Christology', *Semeia* 16(1980) 57–95 at p. 60.

Mark, 'I came not to call the righteous, but the sinners'. It is Luke who adds the words 'to repentance' (Lk 5.32): this significantly alters the meaning of the sentence. We must then be careful not to homogenize the Gospel material.

CHAPTER V

FROM ORAL TRADITION TO WRITTEN MATERIAL

Already in the oral stage of the tradition some of the separate incidents had come together, e.g. there are sections of parables in chapter 4, and of miracles in chapter 5 (4.35–5.43). The material in these complexes was drawn together because it possessed either a common form or a common theme. That this took place prior to the appearance of any of the gospels does not mean that the gospels themselves developed through the material continuing to grow together. There is always some common factor joining together the incidents in any complex, and that gives no reason to suppose that the complexes would necessarily have joined themselves up to one another by some natural process of evolution. The step from the complexes to the first gospel was deliberate and not due to natural growth. It is this conscious step which we attribute to Mark and it is this which makes him more than a collector of material. This is confirmed when we examine the Gospel and find there deliberate signs of his hand; he carefully unifies the material in such a way as to produce a total effect. Some force other than the inherent ability or power of the material to come together must therefore have been present in the composition of the Gospel. To say this does not however determine what that extra force or influence was, and to this we shall return.

These complexes or small collections would present different pictures of Jesus. A catena of miracle stories might present him as a 'divine man' or as the channel of God's power to the church. A collection of his teaching or of his parables might present him as the revealer of God or as the instructor of disciples in how they should live. A passion narrative might set out Jesus as a patient martyr and hero walking the way of God to his death or might turn attention away from the actual event of the death to its soteriological significance.[31] When these different types of material are put together in a Gospel a new whole is created; the three different pictures of Jesus are not just juxtapositioned. The nature of the new picture can be seen only as we proceed. From another angle of approach we can say that each of these collections was held

---

[31] Cf. C.H. Talbert, 'The Gospel and the Gospels', *Int.* 33 (1979) 351–362.

together by a different structural principle.[32] Mark's main structural principle or principles need neither be any one of these earlier principles nor a combination or amalgamation of two or more of them. To hold the different types of material together a fresh set of structural principles would be necessary. Somewhat similarly Schweizer[33] argues that different sections of the church stressed different views of Jesus. Jewish Christians were primarily interested in the words of Jesus, and therefore in Q. Pauline churches were interested in the cross and resurrection as the centre of their faith. The Syrian communities looked upon Jesus as a divine man. It was Mark's achievement to unite these three previous interests and so to create a new picture. Whether Mark worked as consciously as this is another matter. The material existing in Rome may have had these differing emphases within it but Mark may neither have been aware of them nor deliberately sought to combine them. In any case by bringing them together he created a new picture of Jesus. Its nature will emerge as we proceed.

The step from individual items and small complexes to something which is clearly a whole was also a step from what was essentially oral to what was essentially written; written literature, even where it derives from oral literature, is not just oral literature written down.[34] At first sight it might seem as if the writing down of oral tradition was simply an attempt to preserve it by giving it a more permanent form; anthropologists who collect oral tradition certainly think of themselves as doing this. This as we have said was hardly Mark's primary purpose in writing his book, though it may have been a part of his purpose. If his sole reason had been to preserve the tradition there was no need for him to take any care over the imposition upon it of a certain form. Today we naturally think of writing as a means of stabilising a changing oral tradition because for us what is written is less transitory than what is spoken.[35] Yet in the ancient world and today in primitive societies oral tradition is not necessarily regarded as unstable and it may continue in a relatively stable form for long periods. As far as written material goes Matthew and Luke had little hesitation in changing Mark's written and allegedly stable form; 'writtenness' did not for them imply fixation in a stable form.

There are differences between written and oral literature. It is possible to plan written literature carefully and to make use of

[32] Cf. H.-T. Wrege, *Die Gestalt des Evangeliums* (BET 11), Frankfurt am Main – Bern – Las Vegas, 1978.

[33] E. Schweizer, *The Good News According to Mark,* (ET) London 1971, pp. 380ff.

[34] Cf. W.H. Kelber, 'Mark and Oral Tradition', *Semeia* 16 (1979) 7–55.

[35] Cf. Güttgemanns, as n. 10, pp. 136–9.

more elaborate rhetorical devices apparent to the eye rather than to the ear. That is not to say that oral literature may not itself to some extent be planned; a teller of tales will think out the sequence of events in what he has to say before he tells his story. He may also use literary devices but they will be those which appeal to the ear rather than to the eye, e.g. the dramatic pause, alliteration. There are in fact at least three major types of literature to be kept in mind: oral literature designed to be heard; written literature designed to be read in solitude by an individual; written literature designed to be heard. A piece of literature originally composed with the intention of being heard will after a time necessarily become a piece of literature which is also read. At the same time, though it originally had a *Sitz im Leben,* it may lose this and become only a piece of literature unrelated to any sociological situation. Certainly some written material is never meant to be read aloud; it is normally impossible to follow the equations in a mathematical paper without seeing them; legal contracts are not intended for reading aloud but for careful visual inspection. We should not then assume that Mark was written to be read; more probably it was written to be listened to. Few people within the early church would have been capable of reading it; they would have to hear it. It is important then that we should not look upon it primarily as a piece of literature whose main appeal is to the eye. Because it was designed to be heard Mark's use of 'and' and 'immediately' are quite acceptable; they drive the story forward. They would not be acceptable in written literature designed for the eye.

While it is certainly true that oral literature may be intended only for a closed circle of hearers this is also to some extent true of written literature. Few written statements are self-contained or self-explanatory; between the writer and the reader there is always a shared area of knowledge and experience. The group of writer and readers may indeed be very small; scientific papers may only be understood by the writer and a handful of others; the fact that writer and readers have a common fund of knowledge allows the paper to be brief. The oral tradition of Jesus was passed on within a community which shared a common experience of faith; when Mark was written down this common community did not disappear, though it may have disappeared since then. If we are to understand it we must try also to understand the community for which it was written and its members' shared experience and knowledge. If Mark was designed to be read aloud, was it written in order to be sent to another community than that in which the writer lived or was it written to be read aloud to the community in which he lived? Probably the latter, otherwise we should find some indication within it of the new community to which it was being sent. We shall return to this idea of shared experience; in the meantime it is important to look at one of its aspects: Mark shared with his community the knowledge of the oral material; when he composed his Gospel this oral material did not at once disappear from the minds of his hearers; they would remember it as they heard what he had written read aloud. The oral and the written will have existed side by side and the person who heard or read the written will also have known it as oral. But since written material in those days was invariably read aloud, and there is no reason to suppose that Mark intended anything other than that his book be read aloud and never imagined it would be the subject of careful examination in the quiet of the study, we cannot clearly distinguish Mark as written material which appeals to the eye from oral tradition which appeals to the ear. Mark still continued to appeal to the ear. The spoken word engages the audience more directly than the written. If Mark was read aloud and if it has a certain dramatic intensity, as we shall see later it has, then it too will also engage the audience. Moreover Mark owes much to the oral past of his material.[36] The separate oral forms can still be easily isolated. Catchwords are regularly used as they would be in oral material. There is a simple linking together of sentences with 'and', i.e., parataxis. There is the preference for direct speech and predominance of the historical present; abstract or philosophical thought is absent. This again shows Mark's nearness to oral tradition, though it must be recognised that once an individual pericope is inserted into a larger framework there is naturally a change in the way in which it will be understood. It is also necessary to recognise that the controlling factor of the community which knew and preserved the tradition is not eliminated but is still present. Moreover the fact that the oral tradition still continues alongside the written material will imply that those who hear the written material in the first instance, though this will disappear after a number of years, will hear it essentially as 'heard' material. We cannot imagine anyone in the first few years beginning a reading from Mark, 'Hear the word of the Lord as it is *written* in the Gospel according to Mark'.

Finally before we proceed further it is necessary to answer in a preliminary way one of our initial questions. Indeed the answer has been assumed in the last few paragraphs. The Gospel was written for believers who knew the stories it contained as individual stories

---

[36] Cf. W.H. Kelber, as n. 34, p. 28.

before they heard the whole. They came to the whole with that knowledge. The way we understand any book will depend a great deal on whether we already know its content and the conclusion to which it is moving. Although views about the city in which the gospel was written and the year in which it was composed are important yet it is much more important to know whether the community for which it was produced was Christian or non-Christian. If it is assumed that its original readers did not know the outcome of the story before they read it, then they will miss the early references to the death of Jesus (2.19–20; 3.6); when they come to the prophecy of 8.31 they will not know that it was fulfilled; they will not see the death of John the Baptist as a minor passion; they will not realise that when Jesus says 'For that is why I came out' (1.38) there is a double-entendre and that the reference is both to his leaving the village in which he had spent the night and to his coming out from God. Thus the use of dramatic irony will be very different if the book is intended for Christians rather than to be used in missionary work or as an apologetic for those who do not know or accept the full story; the welcome by the crowds of Jesus to Jerusalem is only ironical when we know the end. We have taken up a position on this issue at the beginning because it is so important. This point of course is true as much for those who hold it to have a pastoral purpose as for those who believe it is polemical and written against heresies threatening the church.

CHAPTER VI

THE OCCASION OF THE GOSPEL

We turn now to the question of the occasion of the writing of the Gospel, and by this is meant its precipitating cause. We have already rejected the idea that the oral material had within itself a principle of development through which the gospel form would automatically evolve. I have been preaching and teaching Mark's Gospel and thinking about it for many years and most of the things I am writing here I have been expressing in my regular lectures in different ways, often set in a different relation to one another; in many cases my lecture notes exist only as brief phrases or memos which are expanded orally year by year, and probably differently each year; the invitation to give the Nils W. Lund Memorial Lectures at North Park Theological Seminary forced me to crystallise my thoughts into written form; the invitation became the occasion of my writing. Samuel Johnson wrote his novel *Rasselas* in order to raise money to meet the expenses of his mother's funeral. There is no inherent connection between the cause and the content of what he wrote; indeed we may suppose that he had already in his mind what he was going to write but being an indolent man it took some outside cause to get him to put pen to paper. Most of those however who have laid stress on the precipitating cause of Mark's Gospel have connected it in some way or other to its content. For a long time Mark may have had in his mind the ideas which appear in the Gospel; what was it which actually made him produce the Gospel? It was hardly an invitation to deliver a course of lectures or an attempt to raise money for his mother's funeral! It may have been some tendency within his own community which he saw was leading it astray and which he wished to correct, it may have been some event within that community, e.g. the death of Peter, it may have been some event outside the community, e.g. the fall of Jerusalem, it may have been persecution bearing down upon the community from outside, or it may have been a conviction that the parousia was only a few months away. We must look now in detail at some of these suggestions.

A. It has been traditionally answered that Mark was Peter's amanuensis and that either just before Peter was martyred, or shortly thereafter, he wrote down the stories which Peter had been telling.[37] This can be put, and often is, less concretely by saying that Mark wrote because the eye-witnesses of the life of Jesus were dying out; their death would then be the precipitating cause. One can imagine the situation in Rome after the death of Peter with the realisation that most of those who had seen Jesus on earth were now dead; the elders of the church would come to Mark who himself came from Jerusalem, who may even have been an eye-witness as a boy of some of the events of Jesus' life, who had been a friend of Peter and Paul, and would request him to write down what he remembered of Peter's stories about Jesus. So the Gospel was written. Support for this view is found in the testimony of Papias, recorded in Eusebius, the fourth century historian; Papias, of course, belonged to the first part of the second century and in the testimony which Eusebius quotes Papias is himself quoting some-one whom he calls the 'elder' or 'presbyter'.

> And the Presbyter used to say this, 'Mark became Peter's interpreter and wrote accurately all that he remembered, not, indeed, in order, of the things said or done by the Lord. For he had not heard the Lord nor had he followed him, but later on, as I said, followed Peter who used to give teaching as necessity demanded but not making, as it were, an arrangement of the Lord's oracles, so that Mark did nothing wrong in thus writing down single points as he remembered them. For to one thing he gave attention, to leave nothing out of what he had heard and to make no false statements in them.[38]

Before we go on to discuss this in relation to our present question we should note some elements in it: (i) 'not in order'; this supports the idea that the incidents before Mark used them had lost their data of time and place; there is no recognised order. Strictly we do not know for what kind of order Papias was looking; whatever it was he did not find it; his failure to find an 'order' may have come about partly because the situation which produced the Gospel was already a thing of the past and unknown to him. (ii) R.P. Martin[39] not unfairly translates the phrase 'give teaching as necessity demanded' as 'adapted his teaching'; in the original text it is not clear whether the subject of this phrase is Peter or Mark; but if Peter could adapt his teaching so also could Mark. Later on we shall be arguing that the Gospel was written in relation to a particular situation. Teaching is normally adapted to a situation.

---

[37] Eusebius, *HE* VI 14.6.
[38] *HE* III 39.15 (translation as in Loeb edition).
[39] *Mark – Evangelist and Theologian*, Exeter, 1972, p. 52.

(iii) George Kennedy[40] points to the ancient practice in which disciples made notes of sections of the teaching of their masters; such sets of notes were known as *hypomnēmata*. He suggests that Eusebius here depicts Mark as making such notes from what Peter said in his preaching; later he put these together to form his Gospel. It is indeed possible that written notes were made of material used in preaching by Peter and the other apostles but the suggested process does not quite fit the pattern which emerges from a study of Mark's Gospel; long before Peter's arrival in Rome stories about Jesus would have been circulating and in use therefore independently of Peter. This material would have been available to Mark as well as Peter's stories.[41] It may be that Eusebius knowing the ancient, though of course not to him ancient, practice of note-taking may have assumed that this was what happened in the case of Peter and Mark and thus described it. (iv) When it says that Mark made no 'false statements' we need to realise that it does not mean what we would today judge to be false statements. We are much concerned about accuracy of detail in respect of names, times and places. The Gospels differ among themselves on such matters and Papias (and Eusebius) who knew more than one Gospel cannot have been unaware of these differences. It was not then to these that he was referring.

The word 'interpreter' could simply mean 'translator', i.e., translator of Aramaic teaching and stories into Greek, or it could be applied to someone who adapted and explained, 'interpretation' being given a stronger sense; this understanding of the word fits in with the clause (see ii above) in which Eusebius speaks of adapting teaching. The exact understanding of the word however cannot be garnered from this saying of Papias but must be deduced from a more general view of the Gospel as a whole.

Three other reasons are regularly advanced for connecting Peter with the Gospel:

(1) It regularly belittles Peter. When he confesses Jesus as Messiah and is told that Jesus must suffer he rebukes his master and is in turn rebuked as if he were Satan. He declares that he will not deny Jesus and yet denies him three times. Must not such information go back to Peter himself? Peter bitterly remembers his failures and tells the Christians in Rome about them so that in the hour of persecution they may draw comfort from the fact that though he

---

[40] 'Classical and Christian Source Criticism' in W.O. Walker, as n. 6, pp. 125–155.

[41] For fuller discussion and criticism of Kennedy's views see W.A. Meeks, 'Hypomnēnata from an Untamed Sceptic: A Response to George Kennedy', and R.H. Fuller, 'Classics and the Gospels: The Seminar', in W.O. Walker, as n. 6, pp. 165–171, 176–182.

failed yet he was restored. Other explanations of the evidence are possible. Some scholars argue that Mark believed that Peter and the other disciples were a corrupting influence within the church; they had a false understanding of the nature of Jesus and of Christian discipleship and so they must be shown up in a bad light as false disciples from the beginning. A variant on this theory is to argue that there were heretics in Mark's own community and Mark attacks them under the guise of Peter and the other disciples attributing to the latter the errors of the heretics. Probably neither the theory nor its variant is true, but we must leave the discussion until later[42]; it is obviously related to the reason for the writing of the Gospel.

(2) Attention is drawn to the vividness of the narrative and to the detail in it; this vividness and detail, it is argued, could only come from an eye-witness; the only possible eye-witness is Peter. Examples can be given from practically every story in the Gospel; three will suffice: (i) in 2.1–12 we learn of the paralysed man who was carried by four friends; these climbed up on the roof of the house where Jesus was, broke it open and let the paralysed man down at Jesus' feet; (ii) Jesus, surrounded by crowds, calls for a boat and gets into it and teaches the crowd from it (4.1); (iii) in the feeding of the five thousand the people sit down to eat in companies on the green grass (6.39). This is not convincing as a means of connecting Peter to the Gospel. Quite apart from the fact that the vividness of detail may come from other eye-witnesses than Peter, I have listened too often to preachers and teachers not to realise that as they retell stories they allow their imaginations considerable play and regularly introduce new detail and vividness not in Scripture. This process cannot only have begun since Scripture was written down.

(3) There is the known death of Peter in Rome. Whatever we say about Peter's tomb it is highly probable that Peter met a martyr's death under Nero in Rome. If the Gospel was written in Rome then it is also probable that as an original disciple he will in some way have left his stamp on it.

If then we were to suppose that there was some connection between Peter and the Gospel we must recognize that it will be more complex than the theory under examination suggests. Peter did not arrive in Rome until late in his life and can only have been there for a brief period before his martyrdom. The church there had probably existed for over twenty years before he came. It was a strong and stable foundation when Paul wrote to it in 56 or 57 A.D.:

[42] See pp. 45–48.

it was probably already there when Claudius expelled the Jews (49 A.D.) from Rome because of rioting over a certain Chrestus, which seems to be a corruption of Christ. If the church had existed for as long as this then it would already have heard and treasured many stories about Jesus before Peter's arrival. In other areas Christian communities were nourished by narratives about Jesus; the same would be true of Rome. Peter cannot then have been the source of most of what the Roman Christians knew about Jesus. From the advantage however of his eye-witness position he may have modified, corrected or adapted what they already knew, and he may have added a few more stories. In particular he may have told them about some of the incidents in which he appears in a poor light; converts often see their pre-conversion life in very bad colours and paint it in that way to others.

It is doubtful then if we can take Papias' testimony in any simple way as indicating that the Gospel consists of Peter's reminiscences[43] of Jesus. But there is probably some relation between Peter and the Gospel. I have used the word 'reminiscences' in relation to Peter. Probably this draws more out of the statement of Papias than is actually in it, but many seem to understand it in this way. Was there any desire in the early church for reminiscences about Jesus? What we learn from Paul's letters about the communities he evangelised suggests they were not interested in such reminiscences. Their interest, as the primitive creeds and Paul's letters show, lay in his birth, death and resurrection. Jesus is rarely used even as an example in ethical instruction; though Paul's letters are full of such instruction, he rarely appeals to Jesus. There is nothing within the Gospel to suggest that Mark considered his book to be a collection of reminiscences; he terms it 'Gospel'; we shall return to the meaning of this word later.[44]

In accepting some connection of Peter with the Gospel, possibly as one from whose sermons and teaching 'notes' were taken to supplement the existing tradition, we cannot accept the 'classical' form of this theory in which Mark is assumed to be a native of Jerusalem, the son of Mary in whose house the Jerusalem Christian community met from time to time (Acts 12.12), and the one who accompanied Paul on part of his first missionary journey. This is an imaginatively attractive theory and has been used widely in putting forward ideas about authorship, but it has little in the way of hard fact to commend it. 'Mark' was one of the most common names in

---

[43] This seems to be what Justin Martyr has in mind when he calls them *apomnēmoneumata* (Apol 106.3).

[44] See pp. 37ff.

the contemporary Roman world. All the evidence of Acts and the Pauline letters associates John Mark of Jerusalem with Paul and not with Peter. A 'Mark' is mentioned in 1 Pet 5.13 ('my son Mark') but he is not necessarily the same as the 'Pauline' Mark; the burden of proof lies with those who assume he is in view of the common use of the name. If the author of the Gospel is John Mark of Jerusalem, why is he at times so ignorant of the geography of Palestine? It is impossible to trace accurately the movements of Jesus to and fro across the Sea of Galilee. Sites named as near it are sometimes otherwise unknown (Dalmanutha, 8.10) or are inexactly situated (country of the Gerasenes, 5.1, as stretching down to the Lake); the many textual variants indicate that from an early period the scribes saw these difficulties. Again the journey from Tyre to Sidon through Decapolis (which is east of the Lake) is extremely difficult to envisage.

The young man of 14.51f., who ran away when Jesus was arrested, has often been taken as Mark's signature, just as Alfred Hitchcock always appeared, if only briefly, in all the films he directed. The preceding account however does not read like that of an eye-witness but as one coming from the tradition. In the passage from Papias which Eusebius[45] reports Papias denies that Mark knew or followed Jesus and by implication rejects the suggestion that he was the young man of 14.51f. The identification of the young man with Mark only became popular in the second half of the nineteenth century.[46] In the fifteenth and sixteenth centuries he was generally regarded as a curious sightseer. Presumably 14.51f. contains a historical reminiscence: a young man was present, was arrested and later became a Christian and told what he knew.

There have been many attempts to explain it in other ways. It has occasionally been viewed as an incident invented to fulfil Amos 2.16,[47] and understood as stressing the perils which face those who follow Christ; the escape of the young man would then represent the victory or redemption of the Christian.[48] More often the story has been taken in a purely symbolic fashion. The nakedness of the young man as he flees may be a prefiguration of the death of Jesus; he and Jesus after his death are dressed in the same garment

[45] *HE* III 39.15, quoted above on p. 22.

[46] For the history of interpretation see T. Zahn, *Introduction to the New Testament*, Edinburgh, 1909, Vol II, p. 446, n. 6 and p. 505, n. 6; F. Neirynck, 'La fuite du jeune homme en Mc 14,51–52', *ETL* 55 (1979) 43–66.

[47] Cf. A. Loisy, *Les Évangiles Synoptiques,* Ceffonds, 1907–8, Vol 2, p. 591.

[48] J. Knox, 'A Note on Mark 14: 51–52', in *The Joy of Study* (Festschrift for F.C. Grant), ed. S. Johnson, pp. 27–30.

(sindōn); as the young man escapes leaving it behind so does Jesus escape death.[49] The young man may be a symbol of the Christian initiate who dies with Christ losing his old nature (the garment he was wearing) but rises with Christ into a new nature; he is then identified with the young man of 16.5 dressed in a white robe.[50] The young man may be contrasted with Jesus; the former flees, the latter is arrested and dies; the stripping of the young man parallels the nakedness of Jesus on the cross (it is assumed that those who were crucified were naked); the young man is thus typical of the disciples.[51] More elaborate theories connect the incident to baptism; Standaert[52] regards 14.51–2 as a transition in which the action of the passion moves from Jesus with his disciples to Jesus with his enemies; Mark's readers would think of their own baptism when they laid aside their clothes and died with Christ (cf. Rom 6.3–5; Eph 2.5–6; the same circle of ideas is seen in Mk 10.38f.); they would thus identify both with Jesus and with the disciples who fled; they would further identify themselves with the young man at the tomb wearing the white robes of the just baptized (for 'white robes' see Rev 3.5,18; 4.4; 6.11; 7.13; Mk 9.3); they belong to the baptized community of the risen Lord.

Most of the symbolic views[53] make some reference to baptism and therefore lose some of their appeal if there is no strong baptismal orientation of the Gospel. They also require us to see a strong element of symbolism in the nakedness. Perhaps with Neirynck[54] it is better not to take the nudity as a theme in itself but as an aspect of the flight, the latter being the essential theme. The flight of the young man just after that of the disciples underlines the dangers for those who become Christians; it also prepares the way for the account of Peter's denial.

Before we go on to examine other views of the occasion of the writing of the Gospel it may be as well to say a little more about the place Mark gives to Peter. It is undoubtedly true that Peter appears as one who fails again and again but if we examine the evidence carefully we see that there are qualifications. When Peter argues vehemently with Jesus that no matter what happens he will never deny him there is a final clause to the incident, 'and they all said the

[49] A. Vanhoye, 'La fuite du jeune homme nu (Mc 14,51–52)', *Bib* 52 (1971), 401–6.

[50] R. Scroggs and K.L. Groff, 'Baptism in Mark: Dying and Rising with Christ', *JBL* 92 (1973) 531–548.

[51] H. Fleddermann, 'The Flight of the Naked Young Man (Mark 14:51–52)', *CBQ* 41 (1979) 412–8.

[52] Op. cit. (as n. 11), pp. 153–168.

[53] Against symbolic views see now M. Gourgues, 'A propos du symbolisme christologique et baptismal de Marc 16.5', *NTS* 27 (1980/1) 672–678.

[54] Art. cit. (n. 46).

same' (14.31), and this seems to be an addition of Mark. Again, in the actual story of the denial, after Peter remembers how Jesus had warned that before the cock would crow twice he would deny him three times, there is an addition 'and he broke down and wept' (14.72), and once more this looks as if it came from Mark. In the story of Gethsemane when Jesus returns he says to Peter 'Simon are you asleep? Could you not watch one hour? Watch and pray that you may not enter into temptation; the spirit indeed is willing but the flesh is weak' (14.37,38); we need to note here that in the first two questions the 'you' is singular whereas in the imperative 'Watch and pray' it is plural; the attention is taken off Peter and placed on all three disciples who were present at the time. It is indeed possible that originally Peter alone featured in the story of Gethsemane and Mark introduced James and John alongside him so that the strain, as it were, was taken off him. 14.33 bears signs of Mark's hand and 14.32 leads quite easily into 14.34 as if the two belonged together. If the information about Peter's failures came from Peter himself then Mark has turned our attention away from Peter and towards the other disciples. Is there here an element of hero-worship? Christians in Rome would know that whatever happened at the time of Jesus' death Peter's boast in 14.29 was ultimately fulfilled.

Quite apart from the death of Peter the church may have realised that the parousia was not coming immediately and that the church would continue much longer; therefore the stories of Jesus needed to be preserved. It is certainly true that the use of the parables of growth suggests that Mark realises the End may be further off than the first Christians expected and that he refuses to speculate when it will come since no one on earth knows the day or the hour (13.32); yet there is still much apocalyptic interest in Mark and there is evidence that he expects the End soon (9.1). The evidence found in Luke's Gospel that he was preparing Christians for a permanent delay in the parousia is not present in Mark. More generally we need to ask whether the supposition that the material was written down for preservation does not represent a twentieth century idea. For us permanent records must be written; oral tradition is too uncertain. Would this have been true in the first century in the kind of community which the Christians formed?

B. The theory we have been considering related the occasion of the Gospel to the death of eye-witnesses, in particular that of Peter. Other theories connect it to the fall of Jerusalem and the Jewish rebellion. The first to consider is that of W. Marxsen.[55] He quotes

[55] Op. cit. (n. 15), pp. 66ff. (ET, pp. 102ff.).

the oracle which Eusebius reports about the withdrawal of the Christians from Jerusalem at the time of the beginning of the siege:

> On the other hand, the people of the church in Jerusalem were commanded by an oracle given by revelation before the war to those in the city who were worthy of it to depart and dwell in one of the cities of Perea which they called Pella.[56]

Those who believed in Christ therefore migrated from Jerusalem to Pella so that the city might be punished for its crimes against God. Marxsen points to several factors which could relate the Gospel to this oracle. Such an oracle linked to the fact of the siege and the overwhelming superiority of the Roman armies would easily produce in the Christians an apocalyptic mood in which they would look for the End, and in the Gospel we find signs that the End was expected soon (e.g. 9.1; chap 13, the Little Apocalypse). The Gospel shows great interest in Galilee; Jesus only leaves it to come to Jerusalem in the last week of his life; it is normally depicted as a good place where Jesus' teaching and activity are received with joy whereas Jerusalem is the place of suffering. This both suggests a special interest of the writer in Galilee and indicates that he is writing for Christians in that area.[57] In 13.14 the desolating sacrilege ('abomination of desolation') is easily understood as referring to the sacrilegious desolation of the Temple in Jerusalem which took place in 70 A.D. Marxsen takes 14.28, 'but after I am raised up, I will go before you to Galilee', and the similar sentence in 16.7, as prophecies of the parousia; the Markan summary of 3.7–12 shows a great gathering of the people in Galilee; Jesus will thus re-appear to the Christians gathered in Galilee. The Gospel was written to persuade the Christians to leave Jerusalem and go to Pella in Galilee where they would shortly meet their Lord.

Eusebius is our earliest source for this Pella oracle. While there is no reason to argue that he is deliberately inaccurate at this point there are reasons for doubting if there ever was such an oracle.[58] Even if we set aside these doubts there remain good reasons for rejecting Marxsen's solution. A flight to Pella and a gathering in Galilee for the parousia are not the same. Pella, moreover, is a particular town, Galilee is a large area and, strictly speaking, Pella

[56] *HE* III 5.3 (Loeb translation)

[57] Note here the different way in which Marxsen makes use of the distinction between Galilee and Jerusalem from that to which Lightfoot and Lohmeyer had earlier pointed.

[58] For a re-assessment of the evidence see G. Lüdemann, 'The Successors of Pre-70 Jerusalem Christianity: A Critical Evaluation of the Pella Tradition', in *Jewish and Christian Self-Definition*, Vol I (ed. E.P. Sanders), London, 1980, pp. 161–173, and the literature referred to there.

is not in Galilee. If Marxsen's theory were correct the Gospel would have been out of date in five years and lost its *Sitz im Leben;* its survival shows his error.[59] Most of the evidence Marxsen produces can be explained as easily, if not more easily, in other ways. 14.28 and 16.7 have normally been understood as prophecies of a meeting with the risen Lord; those who assume that the original Gospel had an end in which the resurrection was described argue that these prophecies were fulfilled by an appearance of Jesus to the disciples in Galilee after his resurrection; those who believe that the Gospel was intended to end at 16.8 can still argue that the two prophecies relate to the continual encounter of the Christians with their risen Lord as they go about the mission of the church; he is at their head.[60] We shall return to the meaning of these verses later;[61] sufficient to say now that we accept the resurrection reference. To some extent Galilee functions both as a symbol and as a real place in Marxsen's theory; in 14.28 and 16.7 it is a real place, but often it functions to denote the place where preaching takes place and is then symbolic. Moreover as a geographical location it is not true to say that it is always represented as a good place; it is in Nazareth of Galilee that Jesus marvels at the unbelief of the villagers (6.6); his disciples show as little response to his message in Galilee as they do in Jerusalem; it is Herod the Tetrach of Galilee who puts John the Baptizer to death. Again, apocalyptic tension is not as great in the Gospel as Marxsen assumes; in 13.32 the ignorance of Jesus about the time of the end is emphasised; the parables of growth in chap. 4 imply the continuance of the church for some time; the repeated instruction on the necessity of obedience to Jesus and his words leads to the same conclusion. Jerusalem and Galilee were not the only places which in the relevant period of the late sixties suffered apocalyptic tension; certainly it would not be hard to imagine the presence of the same tension among Christians in Rome after the Neronic persecutions. It is very surprising to find Aramaic words translated into Greek if the Gospel was written for Christians in Galilee who had come from Jerusalem since Aramaic was the language both of Jerusalem and Galilee. The explanation of Jewish customs (7.3f.; 14.12; 15.42) would also be unnecessary. The Gospel then must have been written for a non-Jewish non-Aramaic speaking area. There is moreover a strong element in the Gospel arguing for the rejection of Judaism and the acceptance of Gentile Christianity; the

[59] Cf. J. Gnilka, *Das Evangelium nach Markus,* (EKK), Köln and Neukirchen-Vluyn, 1978, Vol 1, p. 23.

[60] C.F. Evans, 'I will go before you into Galilee', *JTS,* 5 (1954) 3–18.

[61] See below pp. 73, 74, 76–8.

Gospel is for Gentiles; this seems inappropriate for Jewish Christians who live in Galilee after fleeing from Jerusalem. Finally it is hard to imagine the exact situation in an apocalyptic atmosphere of withdrawal from Jerusalem which would lead to the writing of the Gospel. The oracle itself would be more effective in producing flight; even some of the actual pericopae in the Gospel taken individually would be more effective; it is difficult to see why they should be put together into the form in which they now exist as a Gospel if this was the purpose in view. Those who are 'on the run' do not write Gospels![62]

C. An alternative and quite different theory relating the Gospel to the Jewish war and the fall of Jerusalem is that of S.G.F. Brandon.[63] It is important to realise a significant difference between the theories of Marxsen and Brandon. For the latter the Gospel was written in Rome and has an apologetic purpose. Brandon examined the way in which Mark depicts a number of groups within his story. The Jewish leaders are presented as universally hostile towards Jesus, in particular they bring about his death.[64] Though he was crucified, a Roman punishment, the Jewish leaders bear the ultimate blame. Mark attempts to lift the blame from the shoulders of the Romans and lay it on those of the Jewish leaders, and so show to the Roman authorities that Jesus was no favourite of the Jewish leaders. This suggests the Gospel was written at the time and in a situation when the latter were in the black books of the Romans, i.e., at the period of the rebellion and in Rome itself.[65] The historically improbable Barabbas account was introduced by Mark to explain to Rome how Jesus came to be crucified as a Jewish revolutionary.[66] Mark also displays hostility towards the immediate family of Jesus and the original disciples.[67] In 3.21 and in 3.31–35 his family are depicted as considering him mad and he as saying that his true family are those who do the will of his Father; in 6.1–6 the people of Nazareth and, by implication, his family are hostile to him. Throughout the Gospel the original disciples are also pictured as opposing him for they fail to understand him and eventually run away at the moment of crisis. Thus the original Christian community in Jerusalem is shown as failing Jesus; by implication the community in Rome where the Gospel was written dissociates itself from that original community; consequently the

---

[62] For more extensive criticism of Marxsen's view see R.P. Martin, as n. 39, pp. 70ff.
[63] *Jesus and the Zealots,* Manchester, 1967, pp. 221–282.
[64] Op. cit., pp. 265ff.
[65] Op. cit., pp. 247ff.
[66] Op. cit., pp. 258ff.
[67] Op. cit., pp. 274ff.

true Christian has no real connection with Jewish nationalist sentiment.

Some of the material within the Gospel points the same way. In 12.35–37 it is the scribes who attribute Davidic sonship to the messiah but Jesus denies that that sonship is his. In the pericope about the penny Jesus carefully affirms the duty of the Christian to be an obedient subject within the Roman Empire; the payment of tribute to Rome was one of the issues which brought about the revolt of 66 A.D.[68] In the Passion narrative Pilate recognises the innocence of Jesus but has his hand forced by the Jewish leaders who are set on Jesus' destruction.

Brandon dates the Gospel as written after the fall of Jerusalem through evidence which he discovers within the Gospel itself. Shortly after the fall of Jerusalem the Emperor Vespasian had his triumph at Rome in which the furnishings of the Temple were exhibited in procession; the rending of the veil (15.38) can be understood as indicating Mark's own testimony to this triumph.[69] 13.14 is, as with Marxsen, taken to refer to the time of the destruction of Jerusalem as already an accomplished fact.[70] In 13.2 Jesus proclaims the destruction of the Temple and yet those who report this at his trial are described as 'false witnesses'; the evidence of the witnesses is part of the earlier Passion story, but 13.2 is Mark's own statement intended to indicate Jesus' disapproval of the Jewish rebellion and to show at the same time that he did not say he would destroy it.[71]

It cannot be denied that as time went by the Christians laid more and more blame on the Jews for the death of Jesus and less and less on the Romans; this process had already begun by the time Mark wrote and is to be found in his Gospel. The solution, however, is more complex than Brandon suggests. While the Jewish leaders are not presented in a favourable light in the Gospel yet the Jewish people, the crowd, are normally neutral; thus the Jewish nation as such is not necessarily attacked by Mark. So far as the family of Jesus and his original disciples are concerned, they function, as we shall see later, in the Gospel, not as figures in history whose story needs to be told for its own sake, but as examples to Mark's congregation so that the nature of true discipleship may be taught. We can however accept Brandon's view[72] that Mark contrary to his usual custom does not translate the Aramaic word for zealot,

[68] Op. cit., pp. 224ff.
[69] Op. cit., pp. 227ff.
[70] Op. cit., pp. 230ff.
[71] Op. cit., pp. 233ff.
[72] Op. cit., pp. 243ff.

kananaios (3.18), used of Simon, because had he done so he would have set the original disciples, and therefore the Christians, in a bad light. This could have happened any time after 66 A.D. On the other hand so far as Barabbas goes there is no evidence that Mark invented whole incidents and the 'true account' of Barabbas that Brandon gives elsewhere[73] is fantastic. In relation to 12.35–37, the question about Davidic sonship, it is by no means as clear as Brandon suggests that in this pericope the Davidic sonship of Jesus is denied; commentators are divided about this. The answer of Jesus at the conclusion of the incident about the penny is not as unambiguously in favour of the Romans as Brandon suggests; we accept the present form of the pericope as pre-Markan[74]; in the light of Jesus' logion the disciple has still to make up his mind how he will act in respect of the Roman Government, and in so far as this favours Brandon's point of view the logion was pre-Markan and therefore cannot have been introduced by Mark to advance a pro-Roman point of view. It is undeniable that there is some relation between 13.14 and the writing of the Gospel, but the Gospel could by a brief period just precede the destruction of the Temple. The false witnesses are by no means as simple a concept as Brandon suggests; false witnesses belong to the tradition of the Psalms as opponents of those who are good; it is not necessarily their testimony which is false but the attitude which they adopt towards the pious; thus Jesus' words in 13.2 and the testimony of the witnesses at the trial are not necessarily in contradiction. The significance of the rending of the veil of the Temple is hard to discern fully; it certainly implies judgement upon Israel; but this symbolic significance could easily have appeared prior to the triumphal procession of Vespasian in 70 A.D. Finally, in so far as the Passion narrative was a pre-Markan formation, it is difficult to attribute to Mark all that Brandon wishes; if the main outlines of the narrative were formed prior to the fall of Jerusalem it itself cannot so easily and fully reflect that fall. Brandon never carried out the detailed redactional analysis of the narrative which would be required if his thesis was to be sustained; others who have carried this out have not reached his conclusions.[75]

---

[73] *The Trial of Jesus of Nazareth,* London, 1968, pp. 94ff.

[74] Brandon, op. cit., pp. 66ff., suggests Mark supplied Jesus' logion with its present narrative framework.

[75] The separation of the tradition from the redaction in Mark's account of the passion is very difficult and few scholars agree even on the main points; see among others E. Linnemann, *Studien zur Passionsgeschichte* (FRLANT 102; Göttingen, 1970); D. Dormeyer, *Die Passion Jesu als Verhaltensmodell* (Münster, 1974); W. Schenk, *Der Passionsbericht nach Markus* (Berlin, 1974); L. Schenke, *Studien zur Passionsgeschichte des Markus* (Warzburg, 1971); *The Passion in Mark* (ed. W.H. Kelber), Philadelphia, 1976.

Some of what Brandon has argued thus indicates quite clearly a desire on the part of Christians generally and Mark's community in particular to placate Rome, but this is not the same as attributing the occasion and origin of the Gospel to the fall of Jerusalem. From the time of the Neronic persecution there would have been a natural desire to whitewash Rome in respect of the death of Jesus and to blame the Jews. So much of the Gospel however has no particular relation to this problem that it is difficult to see its present content and structure as occasioned by the fall of Jerusalem. We cannot deny, though, that a small part of Mark's purpose may have been apologetic, but it was a small part.

D. It could be argued that a more likely historical occasion leading to the production of the Gospel may have been the Neronic persecution, and this either because it caused the death of eye-witnesses, in particular of Peter, or because the need was seen for a document which would encourage the Christians to stand firm in the face of persecution. In effect we have already examined the former of these and dismissed it when considering the place of Peter in the Gospel. Eye-witnesses are important when historical reminiscences are required; Mark is not setting out to provide the true history of Jesus but writing to assist a particular congregation at a particular point in its history. Was then their situation, to take the second alternative, the danger of further persecution? As we shall see there is a great deal to be said for this and for Mark as concerned about persecution and suffering. But when he introduces these topics it is to emphasise the integral place they have in the following of Jesus on the way of the cross rather than the simple need for his readers to be steadfast. Luke's Gospel would be more effective for the former purpose with its greater stress on Jesus' death as that of the ideal martyr; Mark writes to bring home the inevitable lot of suffering for the Christian if he is to be a true disciple.

E. So far we have limited ourselves to looking at possible external causes which might have led to the writing of the Gospel; the occasion or cause may, however, have been internal. Strictly speaking the death of eye-witnesses in Rome could be regarded in this way, but what is in mind here is rather something which was going on while Mark was actually writing: some pastoral need of the community or some threat to its unity, stability or orthodoxy coming from within it, or possibly indeed from without yet from within some other part of the church.

In this respect a number of suggestions have been made about possible attacks on the community coming from Christian groups either inside or outside it as the occasion of Mark's writing. We shall look later at a widely held view that Mark was writing against a false christology which he believed was endangering the community. We look briefly now at a suggestion of W.H. Kelber[76] for whom the precipitating cause of the gospel was the failure of the false prophets of 13.5b–6, 21–22 to offer adequate oral guidance to the church in the time of the Jewish war. These would have claimed to have the living Lord behind their prophetic words and their words came with all the power of oral material. Mark therefore plays down in the gospel the words of Jesus giving only two collections of logia (chaps 4,13). The 'gospel text reconstitutes stability and reliability'[77] and restores 'the authority of Jesus as one essentially belonging to the past'.[78] If this suggestion were true we should expect a much fuller treatment of the prophets and their errors and not just two passing references. There is moreover much more of the teaching of Jesus in the gospel than Kelber supposes,[79] cf. 7.1–23; 8.34–9.1; 9.35–50; 10.23–31. Part also of the base from which Kelber works is the absence from the Gospel of the living Christ: 'There is a deep sense in which the resurrected Jesus *must not* (emphasis added) make an appearance in the gospel.'[80] We shall later examine and reject this view.[81]

If we have to look within the community for a possible occasion which produced the Gospel it is important to determine what was the community in which the Gospel was written. There are no strong grounds for overthrowing the traditional attribution to the Roman Christian community. As we have already seen the Gospel cannot have been written in an Aramaic-speaking area, otherwise there would have been no need to translate the Aramaic phrases. Nor can it have originated in a Jewish area for then there would have been no need to explain Jewish customs. Moreover the Gospel shows a high interest in expressing God's judgment on the Jewish nation and in the meaning of the gospel for Gentiles. Both Alexandria and Antioch have been suggested as alternatives to Rome. The tradition in favour of Alexandria goes back only as far as Chrysostom; earlier tradition, mostly emanating from Egypt, ascribed the Gospel to Rome.[82] The alleged 'secret Gospel of

[76] Art. cit. (see n. 34), at p. 44.

[77] Art. cit., p. 44.

[78] Art. cit., p. 45.

[79] Cf. R. T. France, 'Mark and the Teaching of Jesus', in R.T. France and David Wenham (eds), *Gospel Perspectives* Vol I, Sheffield, 1980, pp. 101–136 and Allan H. Howe, *The Teaching Jesus Figure in the Gospel of Mark: A Redaction-Critical Study in Markan Christology,* Ph.D. dissertation for Northwestern University, 1978.

[80] Art. cit. (see n. 34), p. 36.

[81] See below pp. 76–8.

[82] Clement of Alexandria as quoted in Eusebius, *HE* II 15.2; VI 14.6f. and *Adumbr. in 1 Pet.* V. 13 (GCS 17, p. 206). The Anti-Marcionite prologue refers to Italy.

Mark' suggested by Morton Smith[83] cannot overthrow this conclusion for if this Gospel ever did exist it was a second edition of Mark. Perhaps the case for Antioch is a little stronger. Peter had some connection with Antioch though it does not appear to have lasted for any length of time; the testimony of Papias that we quoted earlier cited the evidence of the presbyter John and John was a figure of the East; Latinisms would not be impossible in Antioch as it was a centre of Roman culture; Matthew and Luke might be held to have got hold of Mark more easily if it was written in Antioch, though too much cannot be made of this for Rome was the centre of the world and communications with it were good. Against Antioch we may note its proximity to Galilee so that errors in geography would be more apparent; it is not mentioned in the tradition as a possible place of origin of the Gospel; the translation of Aramaic phrases would hardly have been required because of the close relation of Syriac to Aramaic. We thus favour the solution which tradition has always accepted; in its positive favour we note the number of Latinisms in the Gospel and the adaptation of Jesus' teaching on divorce to suit Roman marriage law (10.12). References within the Gospel to persecution and the apocalyptic tension which many detect in it fit many situations in the early Church and are not much help in determining its place of origin. All the early tradition suggests Rome and we would hesitate to disagree.[84]

[83] M. Smith, *Clement of Alexandria and a Secret Gospel of Mark*, Cambridge, Mass., 1973.

[84] Cf. B.W. Bacon, *Is Mark a Roman Gospel?* (Harvard Theological Studies 7), Cambridge, Mass., 1919; R. Pesch, *Das Markusevangelium* (Herder), Vol I, Freiburg, Basel, Wien, 1976, pp. 12–15; H.C. Snape, 'Christian Origins in Rome with Special Reference to Mark's Gospel', *Modern Churchman* 13 (1970) 230–244; J. Rohde, *Rediscovering the Teaching of the Evangelists*, (ET by D.M. Barton), London, 1968, pp. 138f.; Standaert, op. cit., pp. 465–495, etc.

CHAPTER VII

THE MEANING OF 'GOSPEL'

In order to approach the possibility of an internal cause as the occasion of the Gospel it is first necessary to enquire into the meaning of the word 'gospel'. Today it means a book which tells about Jesus, something like the Gospel of Mark; thus when a set of sayings of Jesus allegedly deriving from Thomas is found we are quite happy to call it 'The Gospel of Thomas'. The word would hardly have been understood in that way by Mark or anyone else in the first century church. For Paul the gospel was what he preached; it could be distinguished from other men's gospels; only his own gospel was true for there is only one gospel. If he had been asked to say in a few words what his gospel was he would probably have replied in the terms of one of the brief creeds of the early Church, e.g., 1 Cor 15.3–5; 1 Thess 1.9f.

Mark uses the word several times; his use is different from Matthew who normally adds a qualifying word (e.g. 'the gospel of the kingdom') and Luke who uses the verb, to evangelise, rather than the noun. On at least on some occasions we can be reasonably sure that Mark himself introduced it into the material.[85] This is so both in 8.35 and 10.29. The saying of 8.35, 'for whoever would save his life will lose it; and whoever loses his life for my sake and the gospel's will save it', exists in a number of variant forms in all four Gospels (Mt 10.39; 16.25; Lk 9.24; 17.33; Jn 12.25); only in Mark do we find the reference to gospel. As it came to Mark the saying already had the phrase 'for my sake' and when Mark added 'and the gospel's' he cannot have been attempting, as has been often proposed, to identify Christ and the Gospel; there would have been easier ways of doing that. The existing reference to Christ carried the suggestion of a personal relation with him; the reference to gospel introduces something more objective; the gospel can be stated in words and Christians ought to give their lives for this statement; the two qualifications thus bring out two related but different aspects of discipleship. The verbal and objective nature of Mark's understanding of 'gospel' comes out again in 13.10, 'and the gospel must first be preached to all nations' (here the whole verse may have been inserted by Mark), and in 14.9

[85] Cf. Marxsen (see n. 15), pp. 77ff. (ET, pp. 117ff.); Baarlink (as n. 26), pp. 48ff.

where it is said of the woman who anointed Jesus that she will be remembered 'wherever the gospel is preached in the whole world'. Nothing in 1.14f. contradicts this: 'Jesus came into Galilee, preaching the gospel of God, and saying, "The time is fulfilled and the kingdom of God is at hand: repent, and believe in the gospel".' Belief in the gospel carries with it the implication of its truth which must be accepted.

What then does Mark mean when he commences his book with the words 'the beginning of the gospel of Jesus Christ'? Surely he is indicating that what follows is a verbal statement of the gospel. This does not of course mean that we can work out a full understanding of the nature of the book through an analysis of the word 'gospel'; such an analysis is one aid in our search for the meaning of what Mark wrote; only a consideration of its total content can really tell us what Mark was about when he wrote our book. That the book however is a verbal statement of the gospel is true whether we understand 'the beginning' in v.l. to refer either to John the Baptizer (vv. 2–8), to the Prologue (vv. 2–13 or vv. 2–15), to the earthly life of Jesus as the beginning of the Christian movement, or give the word the meaning 'origin' or 'principle'. His book presents the gospel. Yet it is not the book as such which is the gospel but its content which is an expression of it.[86]

In that sense Marxsen is correct when he refers to Mark's book as a 'sermon'.[87] Prior to Mark the gospel was expressed in sermons or in brief statements; both of these would give some of the facts of Jesus' life and death with an accompanying interpretation. Mark had the inspiration to present the gospel, not as a brief confessional statement, nor as a sermon applicable to a particular problem in the way in which we are used to sermons, but as a narrative about Jesus in which his sayings and the main events of his life are recounted. However although he expresses the gospel through the events of the life of Jesus this should not be taken to imply he deliberately married the Jesus-tradition to the Hellenistic kerygma, as Bultmann suggests,[88] still less that an attempt to do this was the occasion of the gospel; this may have been what happened but the attempt to carry it through was not the cause of the origin of the Gospel. If we term it 'sermon' it is not a sermon in

[86] Cf. Baarlink (as n. 26), pp. 46f.

[87] Cf. W. Marxsen, *Introduction to the New Testament* (ET by G. Buswell), Oxford, 1968, p. 153, and 'The New Testament: A Collection of Sermons', *Modern Churchman*, 19 (1975/6) 134–143.

[88] R. Bultmann, *The History of the Synoptic Tradition* (ET by J. Marsh) Oxford, 1963, p. 347.

the ordinarily understood sense of that word; it is better described more vaguely as 'a preaching', the Word is declared with a particular situation in mind. This in turn implies that the Gospel is not what we understand in twentieth century terms as a biography. While there is a sequence of events in the life of Jesus terminating in his death and resurrection, there is no attempt to discern a development in his personality or to explain his reaction to situations in terms of his character.[89] Nor is the book the 'memoirs' of Jesus, in the sense of a set of anecdotes revealing the hero's character and giving an understanding of his personality and importance. This certainly happens but as we shall see[90] the structure of the book is more closely knit than would be expected in a set of memoirs. If we contrast it with other writings in the New Testament we see that it is not a letter like those of Paul or Peter, a theological essay like Hebrews, or even a set of 'acts'. It recounts acts of Jesus but it differs from other acts which were a known literary form of the ancient world in that the central act is Jesus' humiliating death.

Some further points need to be made in relation to the Gospel as 'a preaching'. (1) As 'a preaching' it is related to a situation. Sermons are directed towards people living in particular situations and deal with them and their situation. We have already been unable to find a decisive external event which led to the writing of the Gospel. Perhaps, then, in viewing it as preaching we should see it as occasioned by the situation of its hearers. Mark writes to meet their need. We have yet to determine what that need is. (2) It is a common view of sermons that in them God is held to speak through the words of the preacher. In the case of Mark's Gospel this can be taken a little further and, as we shall eventually see, the risen Jesus may be said to speak in the Gospel; through his words and actions as reported in the Gospel Jesus lives again and speaks to and acts among men.[91] In 1.1 it is difficult to decide whether in the phrase 'the gospel of Jesus Christ' Jesus Christ is to be taken as the person whom the gospel proclaims (objective genitive) or as the person who proclaims the gospel (subjective genitive). In fact there is a sense in which both are true; Christ is both a figure of the past in the book of Mark and he speaks in and through it as living Lord. 1.14f., allegedly a summary of what Jesus preached, is a strange mixture of words Jesus actually used (e.g. 'kingdom of God') and of the vocabulary of the church (e.g. 'believe in the

---

[89] See below, pp. 118, 124.
[90] See below pp. 129f.
[91] Cf. Marxsen, *Der Evangelist Markus,* pp. 85ff. (ET, pp. 128ff.).

gospel'); this combination makes the same point in another way. (3) If it is 'preaching' it would be wrong to describe it simply as 'the union of the Hellenistic kerygma about Christ . . . with the tradition of the story of Jesus'[92] as if Mark had deliberately set out to combine the two. Bultmann defines the Hellenistic kerygma in terms of Phil 2.6ff. and Rom 3.24. It is doubtful if it can be defined as simply as this; there were a number of forms of the kerygma; the two texts instanced themselves indicate two different forms. If indeed the kerygma is defined in terms of Phil 2.6ff. this bears little relation to Mark which contains neither the decision of a pre-existent Jesus to come to earth nor his glorious return to Heaven. It would not, however, be wrong to deny that there is a union of kerygma and tradition in Mark. Such a union would alter both kerygma and tradition as each was applied to a new purpose.[93] What we would then have would be a new expression of the kerygma which might or might not produce a new literary form. In the same way the Gospel is not just the development of the kerygma as if the latter contained some immanent principle which would eventually and automatically produce the former.[94] Not only were there different forms of the kerygma which might have developed different 'Gospels' but the Gospel of Mark has a more precise situation in mind than this would suggest. Methodologically it is wrong to start with forms of the kerygma and then try to match Mark to one of them. We should begin with Mark and see what kerygma lies in it; what this is we shall discuss later.[95]

(4) Unlike a modern sermon Mark does not begin from and expound a text. His book is not simply an exposition of Pauline doctrine or, more precisely, an exposition of one of the primitive confessions of the church; R.A. Harrisville[96] sees its theme as that of the christological hymn of Phil 2.6–11. It is difficult to fit the Gospel into such a straight-jacket and if we were to pick a primitive confession which it could be said that Mark represents then that of 1 Cor 15.3–5 would be a better candidate,[97] though we shall see later[98] this itself requires considerable modification to make even an approximate fit with Mark.

(5) The Gospel is, however, different from a modern sermon in

---

[92] Bultmann, as n. 88, p. 347.
[93] See below p. 137.
[94] Bultmann, as n. 88, pp. 321, 368ff. For criticism of this approach and the methods of the form-critics see Güttgemanns, as n. 10, *passim*.
[95] See below pp. 136f.
[96] *The Miracle of Mark,* Minneapolis, Minn., 1967.
[97] Cf. Baarlink, as n. 26, pp. 57–60.
[98] See below pp. 136f.

yet another way; sermons are basically oral literature; even if the sermons of some great preachers have finally been published they were not normally composed with that purpose in mind. Material which is to be read, either aloud or inwardly, is normally of tighter and more careful structure than that prepared for speaking. We can say this without going all the way with Standaert and arguing that Mark has adopted in a detailed way the canons of rhetorical and dramatic structure[99] and without implying that Mark was not read aloud, but only studied. 'Sermon' is not then a very exact term for what Mark wrote but it serves to bring out what he meant when he headed his writing with the term 'Gospel'. It is a sermon in the sense of 'a proclamation of the word'; Mark gives God's word to his people; a sermon is the directing of God's word to a particular people in a particular situation; this is what Mark is doing. What holds it together is not a logical exposition of a theme or a text but the events in the life of the person, even if the events are not necessarily set out in chronological order, for it is their significance for the needs of his community which is important for Mark. Their significance will appear as we work on.

H.A. Guy[100] does not regard the Gospel as a sermon in itself but rather as a development of sermonic material. He notes the roughness in style implying that the material was originally oral rather than written and isolates passages which look like preacher's asides for in them an explanation is given of something in the text. But: (1) There is more evidence of careful construction in the Gospel than Guy allows for; we shall see this as we go on. (2) No one denies that there are 'asides' in the Gospel; Guy suggests that at this point the preacher in repeating the story of Jesus would be adding his own comment and that this would be clear to his audience. After the story however had been repeated several times by different people this comment would have become so much part of the story that it would have been inseparable from it; its hearers would no longer have viewed it as a comment. (3) Sermons would be much longer than individual pericopae; on Guy's theory whoever put the Gospel together must have listened to a lot of sermons and extracted from each just those sections recounting events in the life of Jesus; this is stretching things a little far. (4) Nothing in Guy's proposal explains the form of the Gospel; a collection of preacher's stories would have been quite sufficient to meet his theory.

It may be appropriate at this point to say something about a view

---

[99] Op. cit., *passim.*
[100] *The Origin of the Gospel of Mark,* London, 1954, pp. 114ff.

which has been extensively advocated in recent years. According to it the Gospel is best described as an apocalyptic writing having its *Sitz im Leben* in an apocalyptic community. In this way certainly it is directed to a particular situation. H.C. Kee has put forward this theory most vigorously in his book.[101] It is not difficult to find apocalyptic material within Mark: the Little Apocalypse (chap 13), the many references to the kingdom of God, the use of the term 'son of man' drawn from apocalyptic writings, the expectation of the end. Almost all, if not all of this belonged to the tradition and Kee has done nothing to determine whether Mark has intensified the apocalyptic emphasis within it or diminished it. This is a methodological weakness in his work. More importantly much of the material within the Gospel is not related to what Kee takes to be its main drive. If Kee is correct the cross is pushed from the centre and replaced by the end. While in the early church there were many who expected the end to come soon and Mark contains material supporting this belief there is also a recognition that the period before it happens may be longer than some expected. The parables of growth would be unnecessary if there was no time for growth to take place within the kingdom. 4.14–20, the interpretation of the parable of the sower, requires the existence of the community through a considerable future period if the temptations mentioned in it (e.g., the cares of the world) are to be regarded as genuine temptations. In 13.32 Jesus says that no one can know when the end is coming, yet experience of modern apocalyptic communities shows they are always sure of a date; 13.32 is thus a rebuke to, rather than an encouragement of, apocalyptic expectation; this is especially so if Mark has added,[102] as he almost certainly has, 13.33 to the tradition. His addition of 13.7b,8 imply the same; 13.10, which is redactional, lays down a condition to be fulfilled before the end comes. There is singularly little in the Gospel about the life of the believer in relation to the end: many of the forces with which he has to struggle are the ordinary temptations which come to men; this is shown, as we have seen, by 4.14–20, the interpretation of the parable of the sower; the rich man is admonished to sell his goods neither because he will have only a short time to use them nor because they will be of no use to him in the world to come but because the poor need them; the desire to have a position of importance within the community has little to do with the end. If the end is coming so soon what

[101] *Community of the New Age: Studies in Mark's Gospel*, London, 1977.

[102] R. Pesch, *Das Markusevangelium* (Herders Theologisches Kommentar zur NT), 2 vols, Freiburg, Basel, Wien, 1976–7, ad loc.

purpose do the instructions about divorce serve? Indeed the whole great central section (8.27–10.45) about the cross and discipleship almost entirely avoids the apocalyptic element. When the twelve are sent out they are given a commission to heal, exorcise and preach; experience of contemporary apocalyptic sects shows their missionaries as more vigorous in proclaiming the end than carrying out such a mission. Much of Mark's emphasis lies on living in the present rather than towards the future; 8.35, 'whoever would save his life will lose it; whoever loses his life for my sake and the gospel's will save it', has no overtones in relation to the end. Finally Jesus' victory over Satan comes at the beginning of the Gospel, in the temptation,[103] and is not envisaged as a contest of the future as it is in other apocalyptic writing.

[103] See Best, *The Temptation and the Passion: The Markan Soteriology* (SNTS Monograph Series 2) Cambridge, 1965, pp. 3–60. See below pp. 56–8, 70.

CHAPTER VIII

THE ROLE OF THE DISCIPLES

Martin Kähler[104] characterised the Gospel as a passion story with an extended introduction and Marxsen[105] has argued that we ought to interpret the Gospel working forwards from its conclusion. These are useful hints but they require to be qualified. They suggest that the cross is the place to begin to understand Mark. It is true that the shadow of the cross hangs over the Gospel from almost its beginning. However, the real end of the Gospel is not the cross but the empty tomb. Its final message is that Jesus is not to be found within the tomb for he is risen. Each of the three formal predictions of the death of Jesus concludes with a reference to the resurrection. Chap 13, the Little Apocalypse, shows that the end of the story is not the death of Jesus for it teaches that there is a consummation at some later period. More precisely the promise of Jesus in 14.28, 'But after I am raised up, I shall go before you to Galilee', and the equivalent command of 16.7 given by the young man to the women when they come to the empty tomb, together indicate that there is something beyond the cross. Following Lohmeyer some scholars[106] have seen this as a prediction of the parousia which will take place in Galilee. The evidence adduced is however insufficient to overturn the traditional interpretation which connects the saying with the resurrection. It is generally agreed that on both occasions Mark inserted it into the framework of the story. He did not create it but took it from the tradition with modification. The saying is therefore important in understanding his purpose. It signifies that Jesus is risen and is still at the head of his company of disciples.[107]

Tracing our way through the Gospel we can see that from 8.27 onwards there is a steady movement towards the resurrection by way of the cross. In 8.27 the disciples are with Jesus at Caesarea Philippi, the furthest point away from Jerusalem in Jesus' journey-

---

[104] *The So-Called Historical Jesus and the Historical Biblical Christ* (ET by C.E. Braaten), Philadelphia, 1964, p. 80, n. 11.

[105] Op. cit., pp. 17f.

[106] E.g. Marxsen, as n. 15, pp. 47ff. (ET, pp. 75ff.); N.Q. Hamilton, 'Resurrection Tradition and the Composition of Mark', *JBL* 84 (1965) 415–421; T.J. Weeden, *Mark: Traditions in Conflict*, Philadelphia, 1971, pp. 110ff.

[107] See below pp. 73–8.

ing. From there they return to Galilee (9.30) and come to Capernaum (9.33). They then move further south into the region of Judea (10.1) arriving eventually at Jericho (10.46). Hints of their further travel have already appeared in 10.32, 'they were on the way going up to Jerusalem'. They reach Jerusalem at 11.1 and Jesus never again leaves Jerusalem except to go out to Bethany for his lodging at night. All through this journey he and the disciples are described as 'on the way'; though disguised by variant translations into English this phrase is found in 8.27; 9.33; 10.32, i.e. in or around each of the three formal predictions by Jesus of his eventual end. It is also used in relation to blind Bartimaeus who, once his sight has been restored, follows Jesus 'on the way' into Jerusalem (10.52). We shall discuss the total structure of the Gospel later[108]; here it is sufficient to say that this carefully constructed journey provides its central section. We need to enquire now about those who are on the journey with Jesus.

It may be that no significance should be attached to the mention of the disciples as accompanying Jesus. Jesus is all-important and the disciples only appear in the story because they were with Jesus on the journey; they have no significance in and of themselves. This is improbable, for Mark regularly draws attention to their failure both in action and in their understanding of Jesus. They have, therefore, some positive role within the Gospel. What is it?

Recently it has been increasingly argued that Mark introduced the disciples and emphasised them in order that through them he might refute a heresy threatening his community.[109] The heresy may be regarded either as one which the disciples themselves originally held, or the disciples may play a representative role in that the errors of heretics within or outside Mark's community are attributed to them.

Underlying such views is the assumption that Mark is a polemical writing. It is certainly true that some of the books of the New Testament are primarily polemical; in Galatians Paul combats the errors of those, probably Judaizers, who have infiltrated the community; in the Pastorals there are strong attacks on incipient gnostics; the letter of James is in part an attack on a misunderstood Paulinism. The Gospel of Mark, however, does not give the impression of being polemical. There is little of the personal abuse of opponents found in the Pastorals, or even in Galatians. People

---

[108] See below pp. 129f.

[109] E.g. T.J. Weeden, op. cit.; J. Tyson, 'The Blindness of the Disciples in Mark', *JBL* 80 (1961) 261–8; T.L. Budesheim, 'Jesus and the Disciples in Conflict with Judaism', *ZNW* 62 (1971) 190–209. Cf. also W.H. Kelber, *Mark's Story of Jesus*, Philadelphia, 1979.

have read the Gospel for centuries without this idea ever coming into their heads. It is probably a scholars' mirage created by the attitude they take up to other scholars' writings; they are so used to writing polemically against one another that they assume it is the only reason why people write!

If the Gospel is directed against heresy then the heresy itself needs to be identified and those who adopt this view normally argue that Mark is writing against a *theios aner,* or 'divine man' christology: the heretics expressed their understanding of Jesus in terms of his ability to work miracles; by contrast Mark emphasises the place of the cross so that a suffering christology is set over against a heroic christology. It would clearly be wrong to deny that Mark emphasises a suffering Messiah but that does not require us to believe that he is arguing against another christology, and in particular a 'divine-man' christology.[110] Wherever Christianity has been taught there has always been in all those who have accepted it a desire to evade the full measure of suffering which goes with being a Christian. To regard such a rejection of the centrality of the cross as a 'heresy' is to use the wrong kind of term. The playing down of the cross is endemic in the very existence of Christianity. Moreover when we look into Mark's Gospel it is by no means clear that he is attacking a view which glorifies Jesus the miracle worker. Certainly he shows the disciples as failing to understand Jesus' teaching on the cross and unwilling to go with him on the way to it. But some of his harshest statements about their failure to understand relate to their failure to understand the miracles. Both 6.52 and 8.14–21 come from Mark's hand and stress the hardness of heart and the blindness of mind of the disciples in face of Jesus' feeding of the five thousand. As we shall see later he has a positive and not a negative attitude to the miracles and draws important teaching from the fact that Jesus performed them.[111]

These references to the miracles and others in relation to the cross clearly show the disciples in a bad light, but of itself this does not imply that they were heretics or that they represent heretics in Mark's community. An examination of the evidence shows that it is not only in the Markan redaction that the disciples are blamed, their failure was already present in the tradition prior to Mark. Peter's rejection (8.31–33) of Jesus' statement that he must suffer

---

[110] On the use of the concept in the New Testament see, most recently, C.H. Holladay, *Theios Aner in Hellenistic Judaism* (SBL Dissertation Series 40), Missoula, Montana, 1977, and J.D. Kingsbury, 'The "Divine Man" as the Key to Mark's Christology – The End of an Era?', *Int* 35 (1981) 243–257.

[111] Pp. 56–62.

is pre-Markan; the traditional accounts of the transfiguration and of Gethsemane incorporate material implying failure on the part of the disciples. Mark has not created failure on their part but taken an existing characteristic of the material and intensified it. Why should he do this? If Mark intended at least in part to instruct his own community in the true nature of their faith there would be no point in showing the disciples as always faithful. It is their weakness and failure to understand which gives Mark the opportunity of teaching what true discipleship is. The strength of God can only be seen when it can enter into and work out through human weakness. The grace of God only appears when men and women fail. If Mark wants his community to realise that they can be strengthened by God in time of difficulty and forgiven when they fail then he must show the disciples as those who are weak but are at the same time made strong, as those who fail but are forgiven; this in fact is what he has done.

In doing this he followed a pattern in the literature of the ancient world. Stories of philosophers depict them as teaching through the failure of their disciples to understand. A teacher, e.g., Socrates, was generally held in the ancient world to be responsible for the activities of his pupils; if they failed this showed his teaching to be inadequate.[112] If then Mark emphasised the failure of the disciples with the intention of leaving the impression that they were unsuccessful as Christians he would in the end be attacking Jesus himself. But if on the other hand he shows their failures and their subsequent restoration through the Master, then he is not attacking them, their views, or their views of their Master. Mark does indeed show the final restoration of the disciples in 16.7 where the women are told to go and tell Peter and the other disciples that Jesus is raised from the dead. Christian readers, and particularly those in Rome, would of course know that Peter was restored and died 'in the faith'.

Tannehill[113] has emphasised how in narrative literature the readers identify themselves with the characters. Traditional successful fiction has long depended on the ordinary person being able to associate himself or herself with the hero or heroine. Religious literature though has often required identification with failure; this was in part the reason for the success in earlier generations of Bunyan's *Pilgrim's Progress*. In the Gospel Mark's readers would identify with the disciples; but the disciples are represented as

---

[112] Cf. Best, 'The Role of the Disciples in Mark', *NTS* 23 (1976/7) 377–401.

[113] R.C. Tannehill, 'The Disciples in Mark: the Function of a Narrative Role', *Journ. Rel.* 57 (1977) 386–405.

continually failing. The readers would identify with them in their failure as they would also identify with those like Bartimaeus who were faithful. Tannehill is a little doubtful about identification with the disciples because, though the Gospel records the possibility of their eventual faithfulness in the message to the women at the tomb to go and tell them about the resurrection, Mark does not say they ever heeded the message. But did Mark need to do this? Was their ultimate faithfulness not known to his readers? Without it the church would never have come into existence. Mark does not record Jesus' victory over Satan in the temptation; he knows it is known to his readers; if they do not know it they can deduce it from the rest of the story. Equally the ultimate faithfulness of the disciples was known to his community, or could be deduced from the later (i.e. post-resurrection) history of the church.

Three other points may be quickly made. (1) If the disciples were being represented as a group of heretics then we should expect to find a contrasting group of good people. There is no such other group of good people in the Gospel. The leaders of the Jews are clearly hostile to Jesus. By and large the crowd is neutral, but when not neutral it is hostile. Possible heretics are mentioned at 13.5f., 22, where it is said that there will be some who will attempt to lead the church astray but it is the disciples in the persons of Peter, Andrew, James and John who are expressly warned against these heretics. So the four cannot be regarded as among their number. (2) If the disciples were being presented as a heretical group we should expect their heresy to be made clear. When we examine their failures we see that these are too wide ranging to form a cohesive position or pattern. The disciples, and the readers, are not only instructed in the true meaning of the cross; they are instructed also in the true meaning of Jesus' miracle working power, in the indissolubility of marriage, in the need to receive children, in the dangers of wealth. These are not the characteristics of some particular heresy so much as the kind of failures which have dogged Christians down the centuries. There is then no easily identifiable heresy in Mark. (3) Mark depends in the final issue on the reliability of the disciples in handing on the material he has used. He does not indicate any other source for that material. If he attacks those who transmitted it he attacks the value of what he himself writes. His community can hardly be expected to accept an attack on the disciples to whom in the end they owe all their knowledge of the way of the cross.

If the disciples are not then heretics and do not represent heretics it may be that they function in the role of 'ministers'. Are they set out as examples (an 'apostolic ministry'?) to the officials of the church in Mark's own day? If this were so, we should expect some other group would be presented as representing the church as a whole of which the disciples would be the leaders. This other group can hardly be the crowd, for it is from the crowd that people are invited to join Jesus and follow him; the crowd is at best neutral and neither on the side of Jesus nor within the church. The teaching given to the disciples is the kind of teaching we would expect to be given to all members of the community; this is true even of the secret instruction they receive when Jesus takes them apart from the crowd. They are not taught how to guide or direct the community but given exactly the kind of teaching we should expect to be given to every member of the community: warnings against the failure to receive God's word and live by it (4.14–20), explanations that what goes out of a man defiles him rather than what goes into him (7.17–23), exhortations about the dangers of wealth (10.23–31), instruction in the nature of the end and of the time of its coming, warnings against heretics (chap 13). What is said about the need to follow Jesus on the way of the cross is what needs to be said to all church members and not just to some sub-group of ministers within it.[114]

If the disciples as such are not to be regarded as representing the leaders of the community it may be that some part of them should be regarded in this way, e.g., the Twelve. It is the disciples who administer the bread and the fish to the five thousand and since twelve baskets are involved this suggests the Twelve as officiants at the eucharist. In 3.13–19 the Twelve are called to be with Jesus and to go out to preach and exorcise; at 6.6b–13 they are sent by Jesus to preach and heal. We note that in each case the material comes from the tradition and has not been created by Mark. If the Twelve are depicted as leaders of the community then their leadership lies in mission activity. This is clear in the two passages (3.14f.; 6.7ff.), where it is said that they are sent out. Once we realise that Mark has written 6.34 where, just before the feeding of the five thousand, it says that Jesus had compassion on them because they were like sheep without a shepherd and goes on to say that Jesus taught them many things, we can see also that his primary stress in the way he uses the feeding is not on the meal as representative of the eucharist, but on food as symbolising the teaching which Jesus gives; the Twelve are those who pass on this teaching. However in most places the Twelve are regarded as typical disciples rather than missionaries and leaders. At 10.41–45, where rulership is discus-

[114] See now H.-J. Klauck, 'Der erzählerische Rolle der Jünger im Markusevangelium. Eine narrative Analyse', *NT* 24 (1982) 1–26.

sed, it is not implied that the Twelve are rulers but it is argued that no Christian should be a ruler; each should be a slave to the others. Wherever Mark has a free choice in his redaction of the material of referring either to the Twelve or to the disciples he invariably chooses the latter term.[115] He still continues to use the word Twelve where it lay in the tradition but by his emphasis he indicates that apart from missionary activity he does not give any special position to the group. They can thus hardly be regarded as officials within the community.

[115] Cf. Best, 'Mark's Use of the Twelve', *ZNW* 69 (1978) 11–35.

CHAPTER IX

THE PASTORAL PURPOSE

It is now time to look directly, though briefly, at the question of the overall purpose of the Gospel. Two possible overall purposes have been rejected. The Gospel was not written in order to expose and defeat those holding heretical views and forming a distinct group threatening Mark's community either from outside or from within it. By implication a second possible purpose has been rejected: the Gospel was not written to provide historical information about Jesus.

The informational view of the Gospel can be taken in one or other of two ways. The information about Jesus and the disciples may have been provided so that those in Mark's own community should shape their lives in the light of their understanding of Jesus and his disciples. This we might call the biographical idea but biographical in the sense of the ancient world and not of the modern. To this we shall return later.[116] The other way in which information about Jesus might be used is a little more complex. Paul laid most of his emphasis upon the death and resurrection of Jesus and said very little about the details of his life. If those details are ignored the danger exists of a slip into gnosticism where Christ is a myth rather than a reality. Thus information might be supplied about Jesus to preserve Christians from this danger. This certainly seems to have been part of Luke's purpose in writing his Gospel. He stresses his use of material from eye-witnesses and those who have written accounts prior to himself. It is not the accuracy of Luke's information which needs to be evaluated in this connection but rather his view that by providing such information he is fulfilling a valid purpose. However while this is explicit in Luke it is hardly present to the same degree in Mark; it may have been a part of his intention in writing, for he is careful to preserve as far as possible the traditions he received, but it was certainly not the major part.

Mark's purpose was pastoral. He wrote primarily to build up his readers in faith. The ways in which he attempted to do this will appear when we look more closely at the content of the Gospel. At

[116] See below pp. 123–7.

the moment, however, it is only necessary to point out that in saying that his purpose was pastoral we are not excluding views that he provided information or attacked false ideas, but that these did not belong to his main intention.

Mark certainly provides information about Jesus and the disciples. The way in which he has approached his main pastoral purpose through writing about Jesus rather than by direct exhortation in a letter has ensured the need to supply information and scholars have used, and rightly used this information to delineate in some way a picture of Jesus; he did not however write to provide grist for their mills. If he supplied information then we shall assume that he believed that what he wrote was true; he may not always have had as much information available as he would have wished but what he did use he accepted from the tradition as reliable. This is a normal assumption to make in respect of authors who do not declare themselves to be writing pure fiction. It is incumbent on those who believe otherwise to prove their point of view. A man writing with a pastoral aim does not need to provide biographical information. Paul wrote as a pastor yet he gave very little biographical detail about Jesus; this did not make him a bad pastor. If Mark used biographical material we assume he used it accurately, though that is not to make a judgement on the ultimate accuracy of the tradition. Finally we should note that in the situation of the Roman church, having suffered persecution and fearing more, simply to provide a biography of Jesus would hardly have been the most effective way of encouraging Christians.

It is also true that in the course of his writing Mark attacks false views, and in that sense part of what he writes is polemical. But the polemic is always held within the pastoral intention. False understandings of what God has done in Jesus for men and of how they ought to respond to that must be shown to be false and be replaced with true understandings. But it would be wrong to treat the views he attacks as forming a consistent heresy held by a particular group of people. Rather they are those into which faithful Christians may easily drop when faced by persecution and by the trials and temptations of the world around them.

That Mark's purpose was pastoral does not also exclude the view that he was seeking to build up his readers so that they would be able to sustain a period of persecution. It is regularly said that Mark wrote against a background of persecution but the evidence is not so regularly presented. B.M.F. van Iersel[117] has examined

[117] 'The gospel according to st. Mark – written for a persecuted community?', *Nederlands Theol. Tijdschrift* 34 (1980) 15–36; cf. T. Baumeister, *Die Anfänge der Theologie des Martyriums,* Münster, 1980, pp. 81–90.

this in detail and we are indebted to his discussion though not agreeing with all his exegesis. There are three clear references to persecution. (1) In the interpretation of the parable of the sower it is said of some of those who receive the word that they will endure for a while but will fall away whenever tribulation or persecution arises (4.17). Because persecution is only one of three causes explaining why those who start as disciples fail to finish the course it must be understood that persecution is not the sole peril facing the church. (2) In 10.29f. those who leave home and kindred to follow Jesus are said to find a new family a hundredfold greater than the one they left and at the same time to suffer persecutions which will come now 'in this time'. (3) In 13.9–13 the disciples are warned that they will be persecuted and are counselled how to behave when they are brought before accusers. The two stories about storms at sea (4.35–41; 6.45–52) are best understood as the way in which Jesus rescues the community in its time of persecution. Echoes of persecution sound in 8.34–38 in relation to taking up the cross and not being ashamed of Jesus; but as we shall see later[118] this is not the main point of this material as used in Mark, though it may have been its original meaning. We agree with van Iersel that we cannot say that persecution is in progress; probably there has been persecution; probably there will be much more, for persecution was endemic in the early church, but persecution does not dominate the Gospel.

Before we leave the subject of Mark as pastor it is essential to consider a problem raised by P.J. Achtemeier[119]: it is not always easy to deduce from the Gospel what Mark has inherited in the tradition and would appear no matter to what community he was writing and what is directed particularly to the community to which he is writing. Probably for almost any non-Palestinian community he would have had to translate Aramaic phrases as he has done, and for any Gentile community he would have had to explain Jewish customs (7.3, 4). Some sayings of Jesus which he uses may be applicable to a wider constituency but be specially directed towards Mark's own community; some sayings are of such a nature that we cannot conclude they would apply to all communities; we therefore assume they apply especially to his own community. In 13.37 he adds a saying which directs the need for watchfulness to those to whom he is speaking; therefore in giving the Little Apocalypse he has his own readers in mind. He continually draws

[118] Pp. 85–7.

[119] ' "He Taught Them Many Things"; Reflections on Marcan Christology', *CBQ* 42 (1980) 465–481.

attention in redactional passages to the stupidity and fear of the disciples; again it will be presumably some element in his own community which has led him to do this. He regularly makes reference to private instruction by Jesus 'in the house'; his community would probably have met in houses and be taught from his Gospel in houses; they can therefore take this teaching to themselves. Mark, exercising his control over the order of the material, may insert certain passages at crucial points because he regards these passages as of the greatest importance; thus 8.34–38, the sayings on discipleship, are placed at the middle of the Gospel because they are central to what he wishes to say to his community. As we work through the material further points will appear. But we must be careful not to carry this too far. We cannot conclude that he was writing to a fishing community because he defines the mission of the church in terms of fishing (1.17). It would be equally wrong to view Mark's community as an agricultural community because he includes the parable of the sower; the parable lay in the tradition and he uses it not because it contains rural imagery but because through it he can emphasise both the dangers of falling away from the gospel and the difficulty for outsiders of understanding the gospel; in any case no countryman would agree with the policy of Jesus' disciples making a path for him through the crop by pulling corn stalks (2.23); farmers would have stopped listening at that point!

CHAPTER X

JESUS AS THE ONE WHO CARES

It is now time to turn more directly to an examination of the content of the Gospel and we begin by returning to a point made earlier. Before discussing the overall purpose of the Gospel and the role of the disciples within it we observed that at least the second half of the Gospel was put in the form of a journey towards the cross and the resurrection and that Jesus went on this journey at the head of his disciples. One image used in this connection is that of shepherd and sheep. In the saying of 14.28, whose content is repeated in 16.7, Jesus says that after he is raised up he will go before the disciples into Galilee. The context of the first appearance of the saying is Jesus' prophecy to the disciples that they will all fail him at the moment of his arrest 'for it is written "I will strike the shepherd and the sheep will be scattered".' (14.27). Jesus is the shepherd and the disciples are the sheep. It is generally agreed that this reference in 14.27b to the shepherd and the sheep comes from Mark, as of course do 14.28 and 16.7 though in both the latter cases Mark is probably using a saying from the tradition. The reference to Jesus going before the disciples takes us back to 10.32 where the same word is used and it is said Jesus goes on ahead of them on the way to Jerusalem.

The image of shepherd and sheep is common in the Old Testament and was used both in respect of God and of the leaders of the people as shepherd or shepherds of Israel; Israel of course were the sheep. The image is picked up in the New Testament with Jesus or the ministers of the church as shepherd or shepherds (Jn 10.1ff.; 21.16; Acts 20.28f.; Eph 4.11; 1 Pet 2.25; 5.2f.; Heb 13.20; Rev 7.17; 12.5; 19.15). Shepherd and sheep, however, hardly accord with our ideas of pilgrimages and journeys, but in ancient days the shepherd went at the head of the flock and did not drive it from behind with his dogs. Jesus then steps out ahead of his sheep whom he calls after him on the way to the cross.

The image is used at one other point in the Gospel and again it is in a redactional verse; in 6.34 Mark says that Jesus saw a great throng and had compassion on them because they were like sheep without a shepherd; he then teaches and feeds them. Here again Jesus is the shepherd; the sheep are the crowd. On this occasion the crowd is not the indifferent mass of humanity, let alone those who are hostile to Jesus, but the people of God. So Jesus as shepherd is shepherd to the flock which is the church.

A related image is that of the family. In 3.31–35 Jesus, informed that his family are outside the house in which he is teaching, replies that those who do the will of God are his brothers, sisters and mothers. The same idea re-appears in 10.28–30 where after Peter has claimed that the disciples have left everything and followed him Jesus says that those who have done so will receive in this present life, brothers, sisters and mothers, that is, they will become members of a new family. In each case a special place is given to Jesus: in 3.31–35 those who do God's will become not just brothers and sisters of one another, but brothers and sisters of Jesus; in 10.29 those who have followed Jesus, and not just those who are good and faithful Jews, are members of the new family. There is perhaps little sense here of movement and pilgrimage but there is challenge in that those who would be brothers and sisters of Jesus must do the will of God and there is reward in that those who become members of the family enter into a new and living fellowship with one another.

The image of shepherd and sheep may not be one of the major images in the Gospel but it provides a useful key to unravel some of its content. It gives Jesus a unique position in relation to the members of the church and it shows him as the one who cares for them. We commence our exploration of the Gospel's content then with the thought of Jesus as the shepherd who cares for his people.

(a) As one who cares for the community Jesus is the conqueror of the supernatural evil with which the community is faced. Whether we believe in the supernatural nature of evil or whether we regard evil as belonging in some way to the structure of the universe and the make-up of our own personalities the early church looked upon it as a force coming from outside; it was not an impersonal force but emanated from a personal devil who was assisted by evil angels and demons. The Christian must be assured of victory over these supernatural forces otherwise at any time and particularly at the end he may slip out of God's hand and into theirs. Mark continually draws attention to this supernatural evil through the accounts which he gives of Jesus' exorcisms and his victory over Satan in the wilderness.

There are several exorcism accounts (1.21–28; 5.1–20; 9.14–29) and in addition in one of his summaries Mark deliberately draws attention to Jesus' conquest of demons (3.11f.). Exorcism is also one of the main activities of the missionaries of the community as we learn from the accounts of the sending out of the Twelve (3.15; 6.7). The essentials of Jesus' own activity in contact with devils is given in the summary of 3.11f.; when the devils see him they fall down in reverence before him, worship him as son of God and he tells them to keep his identity secret. Jesus controls the demons. He is enabled to do this because in the temptation he has already clashed with their master, Satan, and defeated him (1.12–13). When accused by the scribes that he casts out Satan by the power of Satan he replies that no one can enter the house of a strong man and plunder his goods unless he first binds the strong man (3.27); the binding of Satan is a common theme in apocalyptic literature. When did Jesus bind Satan? In the New Testament the death and the resurrection of Christ are often regarded as the moment of his victory over Satan and the evil powers who belong to Satan (Col 2.15), but the idea is also associated with the ascension (1 Pet 3.22). In addition there is a sense in which it is only at the end of all things that Jesus can be Satan's conqueror (1 Cor 15.24–28). The defeat of Satan which is connected with the life of the earthly and pre-ascension Jesus cannot then be total; it is only complete at the end. It is possible to regard Jesus' death in the Gospel of Mark as the moment when he defeats Satan[120] but it is difficult to provide evidence for such a view. We prefer the view which sees Satan as defeated in the period of the temptation.[121] Mark's very brief account (1.12f.) of this incident does not provide a psychological interpretation of temptation but depicts a holy war. Jesus and the angels are ranged on the one side against Satan and the wild beasts on the other. Jesus is the victor and so from that moment onwards he can deal with those who are demonically possessed. However to place the victory of Jesus in the temptation rather than in his death and resurrection or in his ascension does not evacuate the cross of meaning.[122]

If we view the exorcisms and the temptation as part of a struggle between Jesus and Satan we must however be careful not to allow this to overbalance our view so that we come to regard the Gospel as primarily depicting a cosmic struggle.[123] We have already seen that though the book contains apocalyptic elements it cannot be regarded as orientated solely towards apocalypticism. If it were the cosmic struggle would be much more evident. Most of the Gospel is free from any element of the 'demonic'. Apart from the exorcisms the other healing miracles have nothing in them which suggests they are part of a contest between Jesus and the world of

---

[120] E.g. J.M. Robinson, *The Problem of History in Mark* (SBT 21), London, 1957.
[121] Best, as n. 103, pp. 3–60.
[122] See below pp. 64f., 66–71.
[123] J.M. Robinson, as n. 120.

Satan; they show Jesus as caring for men and in particular for the Christian community. The discussions between Jesus and his opponents do not partake of the nature of cosmic struggle. The blindness of the disciples is either their own fault or results from a temporary hardening of their minds by God; the faults against which they have to contend are their unwillingness to deny themselves and to take up their crosses. In the interpretation of the parable of the sower (4.14–20) it is only one group whose failure is associated with the activity of Satan; the rest are drawn aside by the ordinary temptations of persecution and wealth. Peter in particular is not a tool of Satan (8.33) but behaves like Satan.[124] Finally there is little in the Passion story suggestive of the demonic; whatever may be true of later church views the resurrection is not seen in Mark as the deliverance of Jesus from Satan.

Many today when they attempt to explain the exorcisms tend to 'spiritualise' them by finding in them some victory other than that of a straightforward defeat of personal supernatural evil. Older preachers used to speak of the demons of drink and gambling which could be overcome in Jesus. Others have thought of the Nazi spirit which for a time pervaded the German nation as of demonic origin. Yet others see the same origin for atheistic communism. As we read Mark however we ought not to forget how real spiritual evil was for his community and how important it was for its members to be reassured that Jesus was the victor over all evil powers; to deny this would be to deny the Holy Spirit (3.29–30).

(b) If for some people the exorcisms represent Jesus as dealing with what many today would categorise as mental illness he also deals repeatedly in the Gospel with bodily illness. Mark presents him as one who heals physical sicknesses. It is possible that Mark received one, if not two, existing catenae or sequences of miracle stories (4.35–5.43; 7.24–8.10).[125] It has been argued that in the pre-Markan tradition these miracle stories were used to exalt Jesus as a 'divine man', and that Mark then took them and by using them in his Gospel with its concentration on the cross corrected this 'divine man' christology; Jesus is consequently depicted as sufferer rather than healer. Whatever significance these stories may have possessed in the pre-Markan tradition it does not appear that Mark did anything to denigrate the healing activity of Jesus. It is true that

---

[124] Best, as n. 103, pp. 28–30.

[125] Cf. P.J. Achtemeier, 'Towards the Isolation of Pre-Markan Miracle Catenae', *JBL* 89 (1970) 265–91. 'The Origin and Function of the Pre-Markan Miracle Catenae', *JBL* 91 (1972) 198–221.

he draws spiritual significance from them but he does nothing to belittle Jesus as a healer.[126]

(i) He presents Jesus as one who rises from the dead; if healings are acts of divine men, must not rising again be seen as an even greater act? If the healings are depicted in the context of the cross the cross itself is depicted in the context of the resurrection. In his three formal predictions of the death and resurrection of Jesus Mark uses a word which indicates that Jesus would rise rather than one which says that God will raise him. Thus he stresses the power of Jesus. (ii) Healing was an activity of many of the early Christians and one which was widely approved; Paul lists healing among the charismatic gifts and it is not a gift which he plays down as he does glossolalia. Thus if Mark were wishing to attack the concept of Jesus as healer he would have had to present his case more clearly. (iii) In 9.28f., after the failure of the disciples to heal the boy who had a dumb spirit, Jesus instructs them privately in how to heal; this can only be through prayer. These two verses are redactional and Mark would not have written them if healing were not important for the early church; if the church is expected to heal then surely Jesus can be legitimately presented as a healer. (iv) The accounts of the miracles occupy well over one quarter of the whole extent of the Gospel. If Mark had thought them wrong-headed he could easily have eliminated some of them and given others a less prominent position. (v) Mark refers to them in the summaries he wrote; he therefore deliberately and explicitly draws his readers' attention to them in a positive manner. (vi) As we shall see when we glance briefly at a few of the miracles, Mark uses them to bring out what Jesus can do for his people and how he cares for them. He might have related the miracles to the end as 'signs' (cf. Lk 4.18–21; 11.20 = Mt 12.28; Lk 10.8f. = Mt 10.7f.; in Mk 6.7–13 the disciples heal and preach repentance rather than the kingdom).[127] By not so relating them he gives them a more normal position in the life of the church and of Jesus. By rarely

9,28

[126] Cf. Best, 'The Miracles in Mark', *Review and Expositor* 75 (1978) 539–554; D.A. Koch, *Die Bedeutung der Wundererzählungen für die Christologie des Markusevangeliums* (Berlin: de Gruyter, 1975) pp. 8–12; L. Schenke, *Die Wundererzählungen des Markusevangeliums* (Stuttgart: Katholisches Bibelwerk, 1974), pp. 383–385; G. Theissen, *Unchristliche Wundergeschichte,* (Studien zum Neuen Testament 8, Gütersloh: Gerd Mohn, 1974) *passim;* T. Snoy, 'Les miracles dans l'évangile de Marc'. *Revue Theologique de Louvain,* III and IV (1973), 58–101; K. Kertelge, *Die Wunder Jesu in Markusevangelium* (Studien zum Alten Neuen Testament, 23, Munich: Kösel-Verlag, 1970), pp. 30–38; K. Tagawa, *Miracles et Évangile* (Paris: Press Universitaires de France, 1966) pp. 75–78; T.A. Burkill, 'The Notion of Miracle with Special Reference to Saint Mark's Gospel', *ZNW* 50 (1959) 33–48.

[127] S. Schulz, *Die Stunde der Botschaft,* 2nd edn., Hamburg, 1970, p. 70.

giving the names of those who are healed he makes their application to the church easier. They are thus used positively and not negatively.

On the other hand Mark does not present Jesus primarily as miracle worker. (i) Almost all the miracles are found in the first half of the Gospel and are succeeded by the detailed teaching on the death of Jesus and discipleship. This arrangement symbolises the position of many in his community; they have been attracted by the charismatic activity of Christian missionaries and have heard about the wonder-working activity of Jesus; they now need to move on from this and learn to tread the full road of discipleship, which is the way of the cross. (ii) If Mark emphasises, as he does, the amazement of those who see the miracles he stresses equally, if not more, the failure of the crowd and of the disciples to understand them. When Jesus heals the demoniac in the country of the Gerasenes the people beg him to leave their area; the unbelief of the disciples in relation to the two miracles on the lake is stressed (4.35–41; 6.45–52); twice the failure of the disciples to understand the loaves is brought home in verses written by Mark (6.52; 8.14–21). (iii) There is the important incident where Jesus returns to his own home village and finds that because the people have no faith he is able to heal only a few sick people and he is said to marvel at their unbelief (6.1–6). Surely this is in some way a parable of Mark's own community; its members are unwilling to accept Jesus' healing power; he ought to be at home most of all with them and they ought most easily to respond to him and yet this is not so. To conclude, we cannot accept the view that Mark contests the miraculous activity of Jesus and attempts to play it down; instead he emphasises Jesus as healer; the members of his own community can thus look to Jesus for healing. The miracles are 'Christ in his present availability'.[128]

Finally, Jesus as presented by Mark in the miracles is thus what we would term a 'charismatic'; the community needs to accept him as such and to realise that through him God still heals their ills.

(c) While physical healing was practised by the early church and by Jesus, Mark does not see the miracles as testimonies only to the healing power of Jesus over the body; he discerns within them and the other miracles another dimension and so uses them to reveal more of what Christ can do.

He employs a Greek word *sōzein* which means both 'save' and 'heal'. It carries this double significance in a number of healing

---

[128] R.P. Martin, as n. 39, p. 176.

stories, in particular in the interlocking stories of the woman with the issue of blood and Jairus' daughter. At 5.23 it is linked with the word 'live'; at 5.34 and 10.52 it is said that 'faith' has saved or healed a person; at 6.56 (a clear redactional passage for it is in a Markan summary) the sick touch the clothes of Jesus and are healed or saved (cf. 5.28). The close association of 'save', 'faith' and 'life', three of the great soteriological words of the early church, imply that Mark sees much more than physical healing in the significance of the miracles of Jesus. This is expressed in other ways in other miracles.

In 1.40–45 a leper is cleansed; in the Old Testament and later Judaism leprosy was sometimes regarded as a punishment for sin (e.g., Miriam, Num 12.10; Gehazi, 2 Kings 5.27); the leper is excluded from the worship of God and when he is allowed to return it is only after presentation of a sin offering and guilt offering (Lev 14.10ff.). The same word 'cleanse' is used for the removal of sin (Acts 15.9; 2 Cor 7.1; 1 John 1.7, 9, etc.) and for the healing from leprosy (1.40, 41, 42). Healing from leprosy thus represents forgiveness of sin. The very next incident of the Gospel (2.1–12) reveals the same connection between the forgiveness of sin and the healing of sickness; here Jesus says to the paralysed man who has been let down through the roof of the house 'Your sins are forgiven'; and he says this before he heals the man.

In the two incidents where Jesus is in a ship on the lake (4.35–41; 6.45–52) he delivers the disciples from the peril of the sea; to the Jew the sea was a hostile element, the abode of Leviathan; deliverance from the sea is deliverance from evil. Very soon the ship came to represent for Christians the community of the disciples; they are gathered with Jesus in the ship, the church. The deliverance on the lake then represents the deliverance which Jesus bring to believers in the storms and persecutions which affect the ship of the church in Rome. On one of these stories (6.45–52) J.P. Heil[129] comments, 'the soteriological dimension goes beyond this particular sea-rescue and focusses upon the absolute power of Jesus to save . . . In Mark, then, the sea-walking epiphany of Jesus calls his readers to a faith in the overwhelming power of Jesus to save them.'

We have already seen the association of 'saving' and 'living' at the beginning of the story of the daughter of Jairus (5.23); there is a similar association at the end: Jesus raises the girl. He is the resurrection and the life. It was the common testimony of the early Christians that new life came through Jesus.

---

[129] *Jesus Walking on the Sea* (Anal. Bib. 87), Rome, 1981, p. 173; cf. van Iersel, as n. 117, at pp. 21–24.

There are two stories of blind men being healed in the Gospel. These stories are placed strategically at the beginning and close of the main section on the understanding of discipleship and the cross (8.22–26; 10.46–52). In the pericope (8.14–21) which precedes the first of them Mark deliberately draws out the relation of understanding to sight; in this redactional passage he makes Jesus say to the disciples 'Having eyes do you not see, and having ears do you not hear?' (v.18). There is a similar story in 7.31–37 about a deaf man whose hearing Jesus restores. Since attention is repeatedly drawn to the teaching of Jesus it is important to hear properly. In the story of the transfiguration God commands the disciples to hear his son. Jesus can both open the ears and the eyes of those who at present in the pagan world do not see or hear, and he can also do the same for those within the community who are deficient in sight or hearing in relation to what their faith means for them; as they truly see and hear they will learn to follow Jesus in the way of the cross.

(d) Jesus is seen as one who cares for the community in the teaching he gives. At the moment we are more concerned with the fact that he teaches than with its content; we shall be dealing with the latter as we go on. The most frequent way in which Jesus is addressed by others in Mark is as 'teacher'. More importantly when we look at the places where it is said that he teaches we find that these occur regularly in redactional passages – especially in the seams between incidents; they are rarely found within incidents themselves (1.21f., 27; 2.13; 4.1f., etc.). Matthew and Luke regularly omit these references as they also regularly omit the frequent way in which Mark refers to Jesus as 'teacher'.[130] While it is true as E. Schweizer notes[131] that many of the incidents in which Mark refers to Jesus as teacher or as teaching contain little of his teaching there is much more of his teaching in the Gospel than is commonly realised. R.T. France[132] estimates that 'some 40% of the verses of Mark contain sayings of Jesus with some "teaching" content'; if we leave aside the passion narrative where obviously there will be little teaching the percentage is increased for the remainder of the Gospel.

It should be noted that in laying stress on Jesus as teacher, especially when he does not always give the content of the teaching, Mark is in fact emphasising the activity of Jesus rather than his

---

[130] Cf. R.T. France, art. cit. (see n. 79); P.J. Achtemeier, as n. 119.

[131] 'Mark's Contribution to the Quest of the Historical Jesus', *NTS* 10 (1963/4) 421–432 at p. 422.

[132] As n. 79, at p. 113.

nature. For Mark 'teacher' as a term is wholly inadequate to reveal the true nature of Jesus; it does however serve to concentrate attention on one aspect of what Jesus does for his followers. Yet it would be wrong, though not entirely wrong, to say that for Mark Jesus is more significant as one who teaches than that the content of his teaching is significant. We shall see later that the content of the teaching is important in so far as it relates to understanding Jesus and the nature of discipleship.

A large part of the teaching which Jesus does give is private instruction of his disciples. In 4.11f., a redactional insertion by Mark between the parable of the sower and its interpretation, Jesus, being alone with his disciples, tells them that they have been given the secret of the Kingdom of God which those who are outside, i.e., outside the church, cannot understand; the latter see but do not perceive, and hear but do not understand. Regularly when Jesus has special teaching to give to his disciples he takes them apart into a house (7.17; 9.28; 10.10); all these passages are from Mark's own hand. Their significance becomes clear when we remember that the early church was a community of house-churches.[133] Mark's community was used to being fed with teaching in houses. Jesus whom Mark represents as teaching in 'houses' is the ultimate source of this teaching.

The connection between 'feeding' and teaching is not accidental. In 6.34, again a redactional verse, Jesus has compassion on the crowd because they are like sheep without a shepherd, and then the verse goes on to say that he taught them many things. This is directly followed by the feeding of the five thousand. We are accustomed to regarding this as a symbol of the eucharist, but Mark's introduction indicates that he intends us to see the miracle as Jesus feeding the church with his words. The partaking of food is regularly used, and not only in Christianity, as a symbol of the appropriation of teaching. It is clearly present in the New Testament in the metaphor of flesh or milk as that with which Christians should be fed. Paul says that the Corinthians are not yet ready to receive solid food but only milk and so he gives them simple teaching (1 Cor 3.2; cf. Heb 5.12; 1 Pet 2.2). The teaching of Jesus is as inexhaustible for the community as the bread was for the five thousand. Again we should probably think of Jesus as charismatic rather than as lecturer, preacher or teacher. He reveals what

---

[133] On 'house-churches' see most recently H.-J. Klauck, *Hausgemeinde und Hauskirche im frühen Christentum* (SBS 103) Stuttgart, 1981; J.H. Elliott, *A Home for the Homeless*, London, 1981, pp. 165ff. On the 'house' in Mark see Best, *Following Jesus*, (JSNT Supplement Series 4) Sheffield, 1981, pp. 226–9; Klauck, op. cit., pp. 56–62.

is not understood; he provides supernatural knowledge where there is blindness and darkness.

We should note in passing that there are some whom Jesus cannot help either by his teaching or by his healing: those who oppose him. They oppose him but he does not oppose them.[134] They may seek to destroy him but he does not seek to destroy them. Only his human opponents are in mind here for it may be that he attempts to destroy his non-human opponents (cf. 1.24). He may argue with his human opponents and out-argue them but he allows them to do to him what they wish; at his trial he says nothing against them; he speaks only to identify himself; he never goes out of his way to attack them as he is presented as attacking the Pharisees in Mt 23. Thus he still cares for his opponents though in a different way from the way in which he cares for those who respond to him.

(e) Caring may involve the exercise of authority either over those who are cared for or in restraint of those who would injure those cared for. The former is seen when Jesus calls disciples; the bareness of the stories as related by Mark display Jesus as saying 'Follow me' and the disciples immediately go after him (1.16–20; 2.14); they are in no way prepared for his call nor is their response psychologically explained. Jesus teaches the crowds and the disciples with authority (1.22, 27) and this authority extends over the Jewish Law (2.28). With authority he extends forgiveness to sinners (2.10). His protecting authority is seen in the way he treats demons; at his command they leave those whom they torment (1.25). He protects his disciples by commanding the storm to be still (4.39).

(f) The significance of the care of Jesus for the community is summarised and stressed in 10.45, 'The Son of Man came not to be served but to serve and to give his life as a ransom for many'. This saying, placed at a crucial transition within the Gospel, is the climax to the special section in which Jesus sets out again and again the necessity of his own suffering and death and the need for the disciples to follow him in humility and suffering; thereafter it only remains for him to go on into Jerusalem and die. The care of Jesus for the community is emphatically underlined in the word 'serve'; we then move forward directly to the understanding of his death, a ransom. Up to 10.45 the emphasis lay on the care of Jesus for the community expressed in the word 'serve'; from 10.45 onwards we are occupied with the central act of his care, namely his death.

[134] Cf. R.C. Tannehill, as n. 30, at p. 78.

Curiously we can turn this round another way. He died and rose and therefore is alive; it is because he is alive that he can now care for the community; he could not do this if he were dead or isolated from the community. Thus that section of the Gospel which precedes 10.45 tells us of the care of Jesus for the community as it is exercised in the present, i.e., Mark's present, and the section which follows 10.45 tells of the death he died and its meaning for the community. It is as if Jesus were alive all through the first part of the Gospel; he comes to men in his words and in his deeds; he instructs them in the meaning of discipleship and of his own life and death and he ministers to their needs, defending them from evil and delivering them from their spiritual and physical illnesses. Whereas in Acts Luke sets out the Spirit as the guide and aid of men in the period after the ascension, Mark has little to say about the Spirit; it is Jesus himself who is alive and who is therefore the guide and aid of the community.

This brings us on to consider the death of Jesus and its meaning for the community and we shall turn to this shortly.[135]

(g) Before doing so we must see one other way in which Jesus cares for the community; the ultimate future is in God's hands through Jesus. Arraigned before the High Priest Jesus proclaims that the High Priest will see him sitting at the right hand of power and coming with the clouds of heaven (14.62). The future lies with Jesus and not with earthly authorities. It might seem anyone could say this who believed in the eternal rule of God; Mark however depicts a consummation of which Jesus is the centre. The Son of man will come in clouds with great power and glory (13.26). Then he will be ashamed of those who have betrayed and denied him but will receive those who have been faithful (8.38 and 9.1). Jesus will thus come again some day to his people, and they will be with him for ever. The immediacy of his parousia, as we have already seen,[136] is not however stressed.

[135] See below, chapter xi
[136] See above, pp. 41–3.

CHAPTER XI

THE PASSION

That Mark brings home what Jesus does for his community should not lead to the wrong conclusion that Jesus is at their disposal ready to heal their sicknesses, individual or those of society, or to treat their sorrows. The Markan Jesus is not a tamed Jesus always available to solve believers' problems. He is the Jesus of the cross for whom problems are not just difficulties to be solved ('let this cup pass from me') but concerns to be lived into and through and which may have no happy issue beyond them.

The death of Jesus broods over the entire Gospel. It first becomes explicit at 3.6 where, after a series of controversies between Jesus and the Jewish leaders, the Pharisees and the Herodians take counsel together how they may eliminate him. It was however already probably implicit in the very first incident in which Jesus is involved, his baptism. Whether we take the words, 'You are my beloved Son; with you I am well pleased', as based on the words of the suffering servant in Isaiah or on the words of Abraham to Isaac when he took him away to sacrifice him the thought of death is present. In any case the Christian community for whom Mark was writing knew that Jesus' life ended with his execution at Jerusalem. The first readers of the Gospel before they heard it knew its content, not only the individual paragraphs but also its end, the death and resurrection of Jesus.

Jesus' death is dealt with more precisely in 8.27–10.45 where we have the predictions that he will suffer and die (8.31; 9.12, 31; 10.33f.). In these passages Mark is apparently using an early formula or formulae. Three of them have the same structure; of these the simplest is 9.31, 'The son of man will be delivered into the hands of men and they will kill him; and when he is killed, after three days he will rise'. We note in this the use of 'kill' rather than 'crucify'; 'after three days' is used instead of the more normal 'on the third day' and 'he will rise' instead of the customary 'he will be raised'. These three phrases indicate the early age of the formula and therefore its pre-Markan nature. In 8.31 and 10.33f. this simple form is developed with further detail. Indeed the three forms probably existed prior to Mark and he has used each as it suited him. 8.31 would already have been linked to the rebuke to Peter in the pre-Markan material. 10.33f. reads like a brief sum-

9:31

mary of the passion account and may have been used in some liturgical context in relation to the death of Jesus. 9.31 is so simple that it is unlikely Mark stripped down the formula to create it. Note in passing that each of these three predictions finishes with a reference to the resurrection. Although 9.12, 'it is written of the Son of man that he shall suffer many things and be treated with contempt', has no such explicit reference it is set in the context of the transfiguration where we see the exalted Christ. There is also attached to it a reference to Elijah as suffering at the hands of men and in the story of the transfiguration Elijah has been seen to be alive; so it may be assumed that though Jesus suffers he will live again. The importance for Mark of the death of Jesus is brought out not only by these four formal predictions but also by the material with which they are associated.

The first, 8.31, is set in the context of Peter's rebuke to Jesus for saying that he will suffer and Jesus' corresponding rebuke to Peter implying that Peter does not understand the need for Jesus' death and therefore is grievously at fault. The second, 9.12, has in its context references to the fear (9.6) and questioning among themselves (9.10) of the disciples. The third, 9.31, is followed by their failure to understand Jesus and their fear to ask him (v.32). The fourth, 10.33f., is preceded by the statement that Jesus was going to Jerusalem and walking ahead of the disciples; they are amazed and afraid as they follow. It is not easy for disciples, or Christians, to grasp the need for Jesus' death and understand its meaning.

If Jesus is able to heal the sick and raise the dead why should he have to suffer? If he is the son of man (we do not need to discuss whether he thought he was the son of man or not; for Mark he is the son of man) why should such an apocalyptic figure need to suffer? (We note that the predictions are phrased, not as we should expect in the first person, but in the third person in relation to the son of man.) In these and other ways the contrast between what Jesus is and what happens to him is drawn out. The irony of the contrast becomes explicit in the mockery of the priests and scribes as he hangs on the cross: 'He saved others; he cannot save himself' (15.31). Mark and his readers know he has saved them; yet he himself died.

It is perhaps important to say here a little about a passage already mentioned[137] but not discussed in detail, namely, the healing of the blind man in two stages (8.22–26). In this story Jesus apparently fails at the first attempt for the man's sight is only

[137] See p. 62.

partially restored; at the second attempt he succeeds fully and the man sees properly. If the restoration of sight symbolises the opening of the understanding to truth then in its present context this miracle suggests that an understanding of the death of Jesus, and we may add in anticipation an understanding of discipleship, may come in more than one stage. When Jesus asks Peter who he is Peter says that he is the Messiah. This is partial sight. Peter recognises that Jesus is someone of unique importance and places him in the most outstanding category he knows but, as Peter understands that category and as it was then normally understood, it is the category of one who rules, and rules by force rather than love; this is not what Jesus is. Thus Peter sees only partially; it is only as the story develops beyond the resurrection that he sees fully.

Wherein then lie the necessity and meaning of the death of Jesus?

(a) The death of Jesus is part of God's plan. Jesus predicts his own death and it takes place as he has predicted. In the first of these predictions (8.31) it is said that Jesus must suffer; the 'must' is the 'must' of divine necessity, not that of human chance or human political reckoning that defiance of the authorities will lead to their powerful opposition. As we move towards the death this predestined element becomes more explicit. At the Last Supper Jesus says, 'For the Son of man goes as it is written of him' (14.21). In Gethsemane he prays, 'Not what I will but what you will' (14.36). That Jesus' death is part of God's plan is implicit in the way Old Testament quotations are used to explain it: in 14.27 Jesus using words of Zechariah speaks of the shepherd being stricken and his sheep scattered. In the passion itself two of the psalms of suffering, 22 and 69, are used several times: the cry 'My God, my God, why have you abandoned me?' (15.34) comes from Psalm 22.1; the same psalm appears again at v.24 (22.18) and v.29 (22.7f.) in the references to the division of Jesus' garments and the derision of the bystanders.

(b) The necessity of the death of Jesus is also implicit in the meaning attached to it. It is a ransom for men (10.45); without it men could not be set free. The background to this verse has been disputed. It is unnecessary for us to discuss[138] whether the saying goes back to Jesus and whether it depends directly on Isaiah 53. Probably we should see in it an example of the relation of the one to the many which runs right through Jewish thought: the many benefit through what happens to the one. The nearest actual parallel is 4 Macc 17.21f. where it says of the Jewish martyrs,

---

[138] For fuller discussion see Best, as n. 103, pp. 140ff.

'They gave their lives as it were for the sins of the nation; through the blood of these righteous men and the expiation (propitiation) of their death, the divine providence delivered Israel which had been earlier maltreated' (cf. 6.27ff.; 18.4; 2 Macc 7.37f.). In some way the death of Jesus deals with the sins of men. There has been futile discussion whether the 'ransom' was paid to God or to the devil, but the saying can be understood without settling between these alternatives. When soldiers in battle have given their lives to obtain some objective it is quite easy to think of their sacrifice as the ransom by which the objective was attained without any idea of a ransom as paid to some particular person. Jesus' death then is the means by which the sins of men are taken away. The same theme and explanation probably underly the saying about the wine in the Last Supper, 'This is my blood of the covenant, which is poured out for many' (14.24). Jesus' death is for others.

(c) Mark gives at least one other interpretation to Jesus' death: in dying he bears the judgement of God. 14.27b is a Markan insertion of an Old Testament text from Zechariah, 'I will strike the shepherd, and the sheep will be scattered'. The one who strikes the shepherd is God; the shepherd is Jesus; the sheep are the disciples. Judgement ought to fall on the sheep who have sinned, but it falls instead upon the shepherd.[139] It is true that the primary interest of this passage (14.26–31) may lie in the disciples but discipleship can only be understood through the death of Jesus, and the view of the passage about his death is in line with what is expressed elsewhere in the Gospel. We find it in a number of references to the cup. In 10.35ff. James and John come to Jesus and tell him that they want the best seats when he establishes his kingdom; Jesus answers them by asking if they are able to drink the cup that he drinks. What is this cup?[140] If we go back to the Old Testament and Jewish tradition we find that the cup is used in two principal ways: to drink it is either to undergo God's judgement or to participate in his salvation. In several Old Testament passages it is said that God reaches his cup of judgement of wrath to men to drink:

> Thus the Lord, the God of Israel, said to me: 'Take from my hand this cup of the wine of wrath and make all the nations to whom I send you drink it. They shall drink and stagger and be crazed because of the sword I am sending among them.' So I took the cup from the Lord's hand, and made all the nations to whom the Lord sent me drink it (Jer 25.15–17; cf. 49.12; Ezek 23.31–34).

---

[139] Op. cit., pp. 157ff.
[140] Op. cit., pp. 152ff.

Jesus drinks God's cup and therefore bears God's punishment or wrath. This theme appears also in the Gethsemane story where Jesus prays 'Father, all things are possible to thee; remove this cup from me' (14.36). The cup is something Jesus does not wish to face; it is more than a cup of suffering, it is a cup of judgement.[141] We should note that by contrast men drink the cup of salvation which is reached to them in the eucharist. Because Jesus has borne God's wrath they enjoy God's salvation. There is one other striking place (15.34) where Jesus is seen to bear the judgement of God;[142] on the cross he cries 'My God, my God, why have you abandoned me?' He stands outside the mercy of God because he bears the judgement of God.

(d) In parts of the New Testament and more widely in Christian tradition Christ's death has been viewed as his victory over the demonic powers of evil. J.M. Robinson[143] has argued that this is true also in the case of Mark. Certainly Jesus is the victor over demonic evil but his struggle with Satan took place in the temptation before his ministry began (1.12f.); the angels and wild beasts denote the cosmic nature of that event. Because at that point he had defeated Satan he was later able to defeat Satan's agents when he exorcised (3.27).[144] Equally the view is to be rejected that Mark regards the death of Jesus along the lines of Phil 2.6–11, [145] for Mark neither stresses the pre-existence of Jesus nor his exaltation.[146]

(e) The death of Jesus entails the rejection of Israel for Israel has not received the one who was sent to it. The cleansing of the Temple begins the passion narrative. Mark has carefully placed this cleansing between the two halves of the story of the cursing of the fig tree.[147] No one but a fool would look for figs on a fig tree at Passover time. Mark knows this for though he says that Jesus looked for figs he carefully adds 'It was not the season for figs'. Probably the story belonged in the tradition to another period in the life of Jesus and has been given its present position by Mark. Mark intends us to see the story as symbolic. Jesus has come to Jerusalem to look for fruit on the fig tree which is Israel. He will

---

[141] Op. cit., pp. 156f.
[142] Op. cit., pp. 100f.
[143] Op. cit. (as n. 120), *passim*.
[144] See above pp. 56–8 for more detailed discussion.
[145] J. Schreiber, 'Die Christologie des Markusevangeliums', *ZTK* 58 (1961) 154–183.
[146] For detailed discussion see Best, as n. 103, pp. 125ff.; cf. also L.E. Keck, 'Mark 3.7–12 and Mark's Christology', *JBL* 84 (1965) 341–358. E. Linnemann, as n. 75, pp. 137ff.
[147] Cf. Best, as n. 133, pp. 216–8 and W.R. Telford, *The Barren Temple and the Withered Tree* (JSNT Supplement Series 1), Sheffield, 1980.

find none and so curses the tree. He then cleanses the temple where if anywhere the fruit should have been found. By the next day when he returns the fig tree has withered. Israel has been judged; the temple has not turned out to be what it was intended to be, a house of prayer for all nations, i.e., the Gentiles. The same idea of the rejection of Israel and the acceptance of the Gentiles comes out in the parable of the vineyard.[148] The owner lets it to tenant-farmers and goes away. He sends messengers for what is due to him; they are ill-treated and he receives nothing. Finally he sends his son and the farmers kill him. The story ends by saying that the vineyard is taken away from them and given to others. In other words Israel is judged; it is no longer the people of God; there is a new people drawn from the Gentiles. Israel's judgement is seen again in the reference at the death of Jesus to the rending of the veil of the temple (15.38); her religion is judged at its centre and found wanting. Directly thereafter a Gentile centurion recognises the true meaning of Jesus and calls him 'son of God'. Israel has failed but the Gentiles are there to replace her in God's purpose. Thus it is through Jesus' death that the Gospel is extended from Israel to all men, and we have not merely a negative rejection of Israel but a positive acceptance of the Gentiles; they are given a place in God's purposes.

Looking back we see that the death of Jesus has not only a place in the purpose of God but it is set in relation to all people who may benefit from it. Jesus bears their judgement; he ransoms them from sin; he brings them into God's community as those who have previously been left out.

[148] See Best, as n. 133, pp. 218–220.

CHAPTER XII

THE RESURRECTION

If that is the significance of the death, what is the significance of the resurrection? We have seen[149] that for Mark resurrection and death are normally held together. The resurrection is given different meanings by the New Testament authors. Luke uses it in Acts to prove that despite his death on the cross Jesus is the chosen one of God; Paul believing that believers are those who die and rise with Jesus sees the resurrection as bringing forth new life in them; in Matthew Jesus as risen is the one who is always with the community: 'Lo, I am with you always' (28.20). What place then does the resurrection occupy in Mark's scheme?

We note first that the Gospel as we have it ends at 16.8 without any recorded appearance of Jesus to the disciples. We accept the view that it was intended to end there.[150] The women are informed that he is risen; they are afraid and say nothing. This seems a very weak conclusion. Let us look at it in more detail. In vv.6, 7 the women are told of the empty tomb and the resurrection of Jesus, and instructed to tell Peter and the disciples. In v.8 they are said to be afraid and to say nothing. We would have expected the story to have gone on to relate how they told Peter and the disciples and that these were filled with joy. As N.R. Petersen[151] remarks it is like sitting in a room below a man who is going to bed; as he undresses you hear him drop one shoe on the floor; you wait for the other to thud down but it never comes. Part of our sense of incompleteness arises from the contrast with the other gospels in which the empty tomb is followed by appearances of the risen Jesus to the disciples and their fear and horror is turned to joy.

Did the women never tell? If they had never told we would not have the story so it must be assumed that at some stage they did tell, that is if the story is taken to be in any way as a description of a real happening and Mark would certainly have taken it in this way. It is not the fear and astonishment of the women, ideas which are common in Mark, but their silence which is the puzzle. Many times

---

[149] See above pp. 66f., and cf. 134–9.

[150] For a summary of recent discussion see R. Pesch, as n. 102, Vol 1, pp. 40ff.

[151] 'When is the End not the End? Reflections on the Ending of Mark's Narrative', *Int.* 34 (1980) 151–166.

those healed are also commanded to keep silent but the stories have become known because there were others, e.g. the disciples, who could and did tell. In this case there were no others who could outflank the silence of the women.

If Mark does not record any appearances of the risen Jesus does this mean that he does not know of any? There are good reasons for assuming he did know: (1) If Peter came to Rome and the Gospel was written in Rome then Peter will have told of the appearance to himself. (2) The list which Paul gives of appearances in 1 Cor 15.5ff. was an early list and we can assume that it was widely known; Mark's readers would probably have known it. (3) Whatever 14.28; 16.7 mean within the gospel of Mark they seem to imply in their pre-Markan oral stage a belief in an appearance of Jesus in Galilee. Moreover Mark has already stressed positively the promise of the resurrection in the three predictions of 8.31; 9.31; 10.33, 34, and the prediction of 14.28 implies some understanding of a risen Jesus. The absence of references to appearances in the predictions is of course in keeping with the ending at 16.8. It is also in keeping with other parts of his Gospel that Mark should not give an explicit account of a conclusion where this is already well known to his readers. 1.8 points forward to Pentecost but the fulfilment is not narrated; 1.12f. tells us of Jesus being tempted by the devil but we are nowhere told that he resisted temptation and overcame Satan; there is no positive affirmation that Jesus in dying did the will of his Father over which he had struggled in Gethsemane; we are not informed that Jesus was ever received back into God's fellowship after his belief that he had been abandoned on the cross (15.34); so there is no need to expect a report that Peter in the end received the message of the young man at the tomb and repented.

Many suggestions have been made to explain the women's silence. The very presence of the women is puzzling. Presumably they belong to the tradition; somebody had to tell the disciples. Unlike the male disciples they had remained faithful to Jesus through the time of the cross; is their failure at this point an attempt by Mark to reduce them to the same status as the male disciples, a piece of male chauvinism? Mark does not appear to be feminist or anti-feminist.[152] Is their failure an attempt to reduce the importance of the resurrection and build up that of the cross? This ignores the strong references which Mark makes to the resurrec-

---

[152] Cf. L. Schottroff, 'Marie Magdalena und die Frauen am Grabe Jesu', *Ev Th.* 42 (1982) 3–25.

tion, and indeed the place of the miracles in the Gospel. His message is not a simple theology of the cross.

We know the women did tell, therefore the last verse must have been put in for some reason other than its factuality. Is it a deliberate attempt, as Petersen suggests,[153] to make us pursue the matter further for ourselves? Is it in order to indicate that in the end the message comes to us not from the women but from the young man who may represent Jesus himself? The message would then be a supernatural and not a human message. We learn of the resurrection, as it were, from God and not from man. Or is it that Mark lacks a proper ending because the end does not come until later? It is not a story which has been rounded off but an open story intended to draw us on further.[154] But to what does it draw us on? Not to the parousia but to the presence of Jesus in the world of Mark and his readers as he was once present in the world of Palestine.[155] By emphasising the empty tomb and the statement that Jesus is risen Mark turns thought on the resurrection away from the idea of a number of isolated and discrete appearances which Jesus made to some or all of his historical disciples. He can be present at all times with all who believe in him.

The message the women are given to pass on is that Jesus goes before the disciples to Galilee; there they will see him as he had previously told them (16.7; 14.28). 14.28 and 16.7 are Markan insertions into an account of a journey which Jesus makes at the head of his disciples towards Jerusalem and death; the journey does not end with his death; it continues with the risen Jesus leading the disciples. Galilee is then to be understood in a symbolic rather than in a literal and geographical sense. It was the place where Jesus preached the gospel without restriction; he may not always have been well received but at least he was only partially rejected. Jerusalem was the place of total rejection.[156] The disciples are now bidden to continue their pilgrimage with Jesus into a new situation, that of preaching the gospel. When they go forth on the mission of the gospel he is at their head.

The association of the new community with the risen Jesus appears also in the twice quoted logion about the temple (14.58; 15.29f.): Jesus is accused of having said that he will destroy the

---

[153] As n. 151.

[154] As n. 151.

[155] See also pp. 132f. for further discussion of the end of the Gospel.

[156] For recent discussion see R.H. Stein, 'A Short Note on Mark xiv 28 and xvi.7', *NTS* 20 (1973/4) 445–452; J.-M. van Cangh, 'La Galilée dans l'Evangile de Marc: un lieu théologique?', *RB* 79 (1972) 59–75; G. Stemberger, 'Galilee – Land of Salvation?' in W.D. Davies, *The Gospel and the Land*, Berkeley, Los Angeles, London, 1974, pp. 409–438.

temple and in three days build another not made with hands. Before we examine the content of this logion we need to realise that the witnesses are false, not because what they say is false, but because the intention of their hearts is false. Mark himself has portrayed (13.2) Jesus as saying that the temple would be destroyed, and the ironic mockery of the bystanders (15.29f.) to Jesus hanging on the cross 'You who would destroy the temple and build it in three days, save yourself and come down from the cross' would be pointless unless the first half of their statement were true. Mark therefore intends us to see some significance in the logion about the temple. Each time he refers to the new temple as being built in three days; thus this logion agrees with his own statements in the predictions (8.31; 9.31; 10.33f.) that Jesus would rise after three days (not 'on the third day'). A link is being made between the re-building of the temple and the resurrection of Jesus. If we remember that the new temple is in the New Testament an image for the church we can begin to understand this link: through his resurrection Jesus builds a new community and he will be with it.

We go back now to the transfiguration (9.2–8); in it the divine voice said to the disciples 'Listen to him', that is to Jesus. It surely cannot be intended that the historical disciples alone are meant. All disciples are to listen to the words of Jesus. A few verses prior to the transfiguration account we read 'For whoever is ashamed of me and of my words in this adulterous and sinful generation, of him will the Son of man also be ashamed when he comes in the glory of his Father with the holy angels' (8.38). When we compare this with the parallel forms, especially that of Lk 12.8f., we see that there are a number of variations and additions;[157] among these we may probably attribute to Mark himself the phrase 'and of my words'; the addition is very similar to that in 8.35, 'Whoever loses his life for my sake and the gospel's will save it', where he introduced 'and the gospel's'; in each case Mark has added a reference to Jesus' words to a reference to his person. All these verses come in the central section of Mark's teaching about Jesus, his death and resurrection and the demand that he makes on his disciples. The words of Jesus are still alive and must be listened to by the church of Mark's own day. We can express this alternatively by saying that Jesus is alive in his words.

We have already seen how Jesus as the one who cares for the community is present in it to conquer evil, to heal those whose lives are sinful, to enlighten those who lack understanding, to be the

[157] Cf. Best, as n. 133, pp. 42–4.

teacher. Thus once again Jesus is viewed as alive within the community and as continuing the same activities among them as he exercised among the original disciples. If, however, he is in the community he is not in it as an equal among others; he is 'at the head'. He leads the community.

A view such as this entails clear and total disagreement with those who see no present existence of Jesus with believers. We take N. Perrin as representative of this view.[158] Jesus is at present in heaven but will return in the parousia which for Mark is imminent. Mark has therefore suppressed the resurrection appearances, left only the account of the empty tomb[159] and presented the women as failing to give the disciples the message of Jesus' resurrection. Perrin takes 14.28 and 16.7, the two sayings about Jesus going before the disciples into Galilee, to refer to the parousia and not to the resurrection. If this is so Mark must have made a major change in the tradition at this point, and Perrin admits this.[160] To make such a major change surely he would have needed to make it more clearly, for 1 Cor 15.3–8, with its list of appearances, was part of the early tradition and well known as Paul's use of it shows. Alternative explanations to all Perrin's suggestions are possible. The absence of appearances may be intended to emphasise the continued presence of Jesus in the community. The two sayings about Galilee (14.28; 16.7) refer as easily to the resurrection whether we take them in the way we have explained or as references to an appearance of Jesus to the disciples in Galilee of which the readers would already know through the tradition. The failure of the women to give the message of the resurrection to the disciples cannot be denied but as we have just seen it can be explained in other ways. The actual message, 'He is risen; he is not here', was perhaps expressed in this way to prevent pilgrimages to the grave. Everyone in Mark's community knew that in the end the message had been received, if not through the women, then through the appearances which Jesus made later to the disciples. Since the resurrection was accepted in all parts of the church Mark would have needed to be more precise in any attack he made upon it. The three predictions (8.31; 9.31; 10.33f.) would lead us to expect 14.28; 16.7 to refer to a resurrection. It is interesting that

---

[158] *The Resurrection Narratives: A New Approach,* London, 1977, pp. 17–40. Cf. N.Q. Hamilton, as n. 106; J. Schreiber, as n. 145; T.J. Weeden, as n. 106, pp. 111ff.; J.D. Crossan, 'Empty Tomb and Absent Lord (Mark 16:1–8)' in Kelber, *The Passion in Mark* (see n. 75), pp. 135–152 and 'A Form for Absence: The Markan Creation of Gospel', *Semeia* No. 12, 1978, pp. 41–55.

[159] Perrin, op. cit., pp. 36f.

[160] Ibid., pp. 36f.

Perrin also holds that Mark shaped the predictions of 8.31, etc. which include references to the resurrection.[161] If the message to the women had read 'He has ascended, he is not here' instead of 'He has risen, he is not here' (16.7) we would be able to accept Perrin's idea more easily; and, considering the magnitude of the other changes that Perrin believes Mark made, this would have been a very simple change even if the message was a part of the tradition and was not itself composed by Mark. Finally Perrin leaves the community without the active presence of God either through Jesus or through the Holy Spirit, for the Holy Spirit hardly features in the Gospel. For Perrin the Markan community becomes a community lacking the living presence of God in the ways in which in other parts of the New Testament church he was believed to be present.

Elsewhere Perrin argues for the importance of the parousia over against that of the resurrection; Mark's readers look back 'upon the cross and forward to the parousia'[162] (Note the absence of a reference to the resurrection). Mark's readers 'are disciples who should accept the full consequences of discipleship in expectation of the coming of Jesus as Son of Man'.[163] Perrin attempts to connect the parousia closely with the passion through the links which have been shown to exist between Mark 13 and the passion narrative, through the passion predictions, through the transfiguration, and through 14.28 and 16.7.[164]

In relation to this approach we would comment that as we have already seen[165] the apocalyptic nature of the Gospel is much less prominent than is often supposed, in particular the urgency of the parousia is played down rather than stressed. Mark 14.28 and 16.7 are understood more naturally of the resurrection than of the parousia and Galilee itself is not used by Mark as the expected place of the parousia. In relation to the three predictions (8.31; 9.31; 10.33f.) Perrin argues that 'Mark has composed them, most probably using traditional material but using it creatively.'[166] If this is so there appears no reason why he should not have introduced 'creatively' a reference from the tradition to the parousia so that the predictions would end on that note. We should also have

---

[161] Ibid., p. 26.

[162] 'Towards an Interpretation of the Gospel of Mark' in *Christology and a Modern Pilgrimage: A Discussion with Norman Perrin*, ed. H.D. Betz, Missoula, Montana, 1974, p. 23.

[163] Op. cit., p. 30.

[164] Op. cit., pp. 22ff.

[165] Above, pp. 41–3.

[166] Op. cit., p. 14.

expected Mark to introduce a similar reference in 16.7. That he has made none of these references strongly suggests that the parousia was not all that important for him. It is true that 8.31 is succeeded by 8.38 and 9.1 with their apocalyptic references and that 10.33f. is followed by the reference to sitting in glory (10.37) but the latter is immediately more than neutralized by 10.42–5. The prediction of 9.31 is not followed by anything which would suggest the parousia. References to the parousia are indeed largely absent from the discipleship section (8.27–10.45), which is surprising if discipleship is to be viewed in its light. As for the transfiguration, as Perrin admits,[167] scholars have been divided whether it refers to the resurrection or the parousia; it is doubtful if Mark would have understood their divergence; he probably did not employ the pericope with either view in mind.[168] It must be allowed that there are ties between Mark 13 and the passion narrative but given the position of the Little Apocalypse as preceding the passion are not these links more simply explained as arising out of Mark's concern to express the greatness of Jesus just prior to the humiliation of the crucifixion? In the light of these arguments it is impossible to sustain Perrin's thesis.

---

[167] Op. cit., p. 22.

[168] 'The Markan Redaction of the Transfiguration', in *Studia Evangelica,* Vol VII, ed. E.A. Livingston, (Texte und Untersuchungen zur Geschichte der altchristlichen Literatur, Bd. 126), Berlin 1982, pp. 41–53.

CHAPTER XIII

CHRISTOLOGY

In all that has been said so far about Jesus nothing has been said directly about his nature: to put it technically the discussion has centred on soteriology rather than christology; this approach has been made because it echoes Mark's own approach. It is difficult for us to come at the matter in the same way for we live in the period after the christological controversies of the third and fourth centuries, and when we approach the problem of Jesus we necessarily do so in the light of these controversies. We want to know who Mark thought Jesus was. The result is that most recent work on Mark has concentrated on his Christology.[169] A second factor producing a christological approach arises from the way in which the Gospels were brought into the discussion at the beginning of the historical-critical method.

> The essence of unrevised Christian orthodoxy was held to be the truth claim concerning these (the chief) events (of Jesus' life), particularly the system of his teachings, his death, and resurrection. This was as true for those who wanted to do away with it . . . The reports about Jesus, it was held, demonstrated or failed to demonstrate that he stood in that unique and absolute relation to God which made him the very revelation in history of God himself. The center of traditional Christian belief was taken to be the christology or the unique revelation in history of God himself in the person and teaching of Jesus.[170]

The Gospels were then searched for solutions to the christological question. A third factor inclining us towards christology may also be our modern preoccupation with identity: we ourselves suffer from an identity crisis and so we push our problem back on Jesus and phrase our questions in terms of identity. We ask: 'Who is the Son of God?' and 'What is the nature of the Son of man?' rather than 'What does Jesus do for men?' Of course who he is and what

---

[169] 'Recent research has shown that a major purpose in the writing of the Marcan Gospel is christological', N. Perrin, 'Creative Use of the Son of Man tradition by Mark', *Union Sem Q R* 23 (1967–8) 357–365 at p. 357. On the importance for Mark of soteriology as over against christology cf. H.E. Tödt, *The Son of Man in the Synoptic Tradition* (ET by D.M. Barton), London, 1965, pp. 144–7; Kee, op. cit., p. 116; M. Horstmann, *Studien zur markinischen Christologie,* Münster, 1969, p. 56.

[170] H.W. Frei, *The Eclipse of Biblical Narrative,* New Haven and London, 1974, p. 222.

he does are related but if we approach from the angle of identity rather than Mark's angle we may be given the wrong perspective and so misunderstand him. It was the attempt to force Mark into a christological pattern, together with the thought that all the New Testament writings were written against someone or something, that led to the view that Mark was writing to combat a false divine man christology with a christology of the cross.

This does not however mean that we can entirely evade the theme of christology. As a major theme in theology today it tends to formulate our questions. Are we not indeed forced into it by the Gospel itself in the question of Jesus to Peter 'Who do you say I am?' Is this not a question of identity? We note first that though Peter affirms Jesus as the Christ this is not an acceptable term for Mark because it carries connotations of kingship; so while Jesus does not reject the term he immediately substitutes another, 'son of man'. To the eyes of prying Roman police this could not be confused with a regal title. We note secondly that Jesus does not say 'I am the son of man' but 'The son of man must suffer many things, and be rejected by the elders and the chief priests and scribes and be killed, and after three days rise again' (8.31). In other words he turns a question of identity into an answer of activity. The son of man, that is Jesus (whatever doubts we may have about Jesus' application of this title to himself did not exist for Mark), suffers, dies and rises. Mark uses 'son of man' regularly of Jesus' activity as the one who dies and rises; he also uses it of the present authority of Jesus to forgive sins and define the law (2.10, 28) and of the Jesus who will re-appear at the end. Again in answer to the question of the High Priest about the identity of Jesus there is substituted an answer about his activity. The High Priest asks 'Are you the Christ, the son of the Blessed?' Jesus answers 'I am; and you will see the son of man sitting at the right hand of power and coming with the clouds of heaven' (14.61f.). As son of man Jesus is to come again. Some of these sayings about the son of man may be Markan creations but many of them were already part of the tradition and at best Mark only extended their use. The son of man is a puzzling concept for us and it may also have been for Mark. It is as peculiar a phrase in Greek as it is in English. In his use of the designation both for the one who suffers and for the one who will return at the end Mark brings out the strange nature of what has happened in the death of Jesus: the one who is to come in the consummation of all things is the one who dies on the cross.

The question of identity and therefore of christology may also appear to be uppermost when after Jesus has calmed the storm the disciples ask who it is that the wind and sea obey (4.41). There is however no attempt to follow this up with an answer about the identity of Jesus. After the second miracle on the lake it is simply said that the disciples are astounded (6.51). The general reaction to his healings is one of wonder. People are more interested in what he does than in who he is (2.12; 6.2f.; 7.37). In the Fourth Gospel they ask John the Baptizer 'Who are you?' (1.21) and the question as to the nature of Jesus is pursued strongly. In Mark they ask Jesus in effect 'What can you do for us?' Emphasis is laid continually on his activity. He may be described as a teacher but the stress lies both on the content of what he teaches and on the activity of teaching rather than on the title 'teacher'. The demons ask 'Are you come to destroy us?' (1.24) and at the same time the bystanders note the authority with which he acts (1.27). It is true that Jesus is identified as the son of David (10.47, 49; 11.10f. [?]; 12.35–37) and as the King of the Jews (15.3,12,18,26) and King of Israel (15.32). These titles belonged to the traditional material which Mark used; appearing in the passion story they serve to bring out the strangeness of the fact that Jesus, the King, should suffer.

The main description of Jesus which Mark uses frequently is 'son of God'. Others in the story so identify him although when he himself speaks he identifies himself as son of man. Thus in his reply to the High Priest he substitutes son of man for son of God. He does not however deny that he is son of God; son of man is the proper term, to which the early church was accustomed, in an apocalyptic saying.

The demons confess Jesus as son of God (3.11; 5.7); we note however that the first demon whom Jesus sees confesses him as 'Holy One of God' and as we have seen stresses his activity, 'Are you come to destroy us?'. Immediately after Jesus' death the first person to acknowledge him is the Gentile centurion who calls him son of God (15.39). When God speaks from heaven he says that Jesus is son of God (1.11; 9.7). Thus for Mark son of God is the title of confession. While we may trace other elements in the confession part of Mark's understanding of it comes from Gen 22; for the reference to Jesus as 'beloved son' (1.11; 9.7; 12.6) derives from this chapter where God says to Abraham 'Take your son, your only son Isaac, whom you love' (22.2). This story occupied an important place in contemporary Jewish thought.[171] Isaac was

[171] On the 'Binding of Isaac' cf. J. Swetnam, *Jesus and Isaac. A Study of the Epistle to the Hebrews in the Light of the Aqedah* (Anal. Bib. 94) Rome, 1981, pp. 1–80; R.J. Daly, 'The Soteriological Significance of the Sacrifice of Isaac', *CBQ* 39 (1977) 45–75. P.R. Davies and B.D. Chilton, 'The Aqedah: A Revised Tradition History', *CBQ* 40 (1978) 514–546 are more sceptical about its influence.

depicted as a thirty-year old man who knew why Abraham was taking him to Mount Moriah and who willingly consented to his own sacrifice. When Abraham holds back from killing him Isaac bids him do God's will. In Jewish tradition the sacrifice of Isaac was believed to underlie and support all the sacrifices which were offered in the temple.[172] Mount Moriah was Zion Hill, the hill of the Jerusalem temple. By so identifying Jesus with the son of God Mark stresses the sacrificial nature of his death. This fits into the concept of sonship held by the first Christians where Jesus' sonship is not one of substance or nature but of obedience; Jesus is son of God as one who obeys God.

15:39

The Gentile centurion recognises Jesus as son of God immediately after his death, because here the sacrifice of the son in obedience to the father is complete, and he says 'This *was* son of God', because he has been obedient. His affirmation is unusual at this point: we should expect it to follow the resurrection as in Rom 1.3–4 where Jesus is designated son of God through the resurrection. Mark's choice of title and positioning of the affirmation is deliberate. The son of God whom he presents is one who suffers and is not to be confused with pagan ideas of divine men or sons of gods and women. It may also at the same time be in Mark's mind the answer to Jesus' prayer at Gethsemane which begins 'Abba, Father' and goes on 'All things are possible for you; remove this cup from me; yet not what I want but what you will.' Jesus has now drunk the cup and done his Father's will. He is the obedient son. It is not surprising to find obedience and sonship set together as correlative concepts; where 'sonship of God' is attributed to individual Israelites their faithfulness, obedience or righteousness is regularly featured, (e.g. 2 Sam 7.14; Wis 2.13, 16–18; 5.1–6; Sir 4.10 (Hebrew Text); Jubilee 1.24f.; Philo, *De Spec Leg* 1.318, etc.). In 12.6, the parable of the vineyard, the son is again one who suffers; in 13.32, where the ignorance of the son about the time of the end is stated, there is certainly no attempt to stress his dignity or status. If indeed there is any point in the Gospel where status is given to Jesus it is that of a slave or servant (10.42–5). Finally we should note the strategic positioning of the references to Jesus as son of God. At his baptism he is commissioned as God's son and at the cross the centurion affirms his fulfilment of his commission. Thus the story is held together at its beginning and end.[173]

[172] G. Vermes, *Scripture and Tradition in Judaism,* Leiden, 1961, pp. 204–8.
[173] Cf. R.C. Tannehill, as n. 30.

CHAPTER XIV

DISCIPLESHIP[174]

It is now time to turn from Jesus and what he has done for the disciples to the disciples themselves. Jesus died for the community; he continues to care for it and to live with it, but he also makes demands upon it. When the disciples in the transfiguration are told to listen to Jesus, that is to pay attention to his words, it means that they are instructed to pay heed not only to what he has to say about his death but also to what he has to say about their own discipleship. This is a common biblical pattern: the goodness of God to the Israelites in Egypt is accompanied by the demand of the ten commandments (Exod 20.2ff.); the ethical section of Romans is joined to the preceding sections which have set out the love of God by a 'therefore' (12.1).

Before we go further we need to recall that in the Gospel the disciples play the role of believers; the Christian can identify with them in their failure and in their faithfulness; he fails as they failed and he hopes to be faithful as they in the end turned out to be faithful. The crowd, for its part, represents the great mass of unevangelised humanity outside the church; the gospel has to be brought to it; mostly it is neutral but sometimes it is hostile; individuals are continually being won out of it into the church.

That being a disciple implies the acceptance of demands by Jesus appears in the very first incident in the Gospel to feature disciples. 1.16–18 is a story stripped down to contain nothing but the bare essentials. Jesus suddenly appears out of the blue and calls Peter and Andrew to be his disciples. There has been no psychological or other preparation. They answer his summons immediately leaving their nets and going with him. But his call is not just a call to follow, it is a call to follow and become fishers of men. There is laid on them a demand which takes them not only outside themselves, but also outside their community into the world. Although Peter and Andrew are later seen to occupy a special position in the Gospel as members of the Twelve we cannot restrict this incident as if it only affected them as belonging to the Twelve. Peter and Andrew function here more generally as representative disciples or believ-

[174] The argument used here is given with much more detail in my *Following Jesus* (see n. 133). Details of other literature will also be found there.

ers. That this is so is confirmed by 2.14 where Levi is approached in a similar way by Jesus and leaves his work and follows Jesus; for Mark Levi is not one of the Twelve. Elsewhere also Jesus makes demands on men other than the Twelve to follow him and be his disciples. The rich man who comes to him in 10.17–22 is called, not simply to abandon his goods, but to use them in the service of God; he is to sell what he has and give to the poor. Concern for the world outside the community in order to win it for Christ is not a task laid on the apostles alone but on all members of the community. Some of course will be set aside as missionaries and either for a limited period or for life be given a special duty towards the outside world (3.13–19; 6.7–13), but no believer escapes this duty entirely.

Returning to the call of Levi we see this duty expressed in a different way. The pre-Markan tradition in chap 2 consisted of a set of controversy stories; into these Mark has inserted the incident about Levi (2.13–14). Jesus returns to the lakeside where he had been when he called Peter and Andrew and again teaches. He calls Levi who immediately joins him. No explicit demand is made on Levi but we find that Levi immediately sets up a feast in his own house to which he invites fellow tax collectors and sinners to meet Jesus. Levi is thus beginning his missionary work.

In 3.31–35 Jesus is in a house with an unidentified group of people who may be taken to represent believers; he is told that his family are outside; he answers that those who are with him are his family, for 'Whoever does the will of God is my brother and sister and mother'. Here again is a demand, but expressed this time in terms of obedience to God's will. The content of that obedience becomes clearer as we go through the Gospel.

It is dealt with pre-eminently in the great central section, 8.27–10.45. This depicts a journey to Jerusalem and the cross, a journey on which Jesus leads his disciples. He is 'on the way' and they are 'on the way' with him (8.27; 9.33; 10.17, 32, 52). The journey falls roughly into three parts each of which begins with a prediction by Jesus of his suffering, death and resurrection and is followed by teaching on the nature of discipleship. Thus in each part discipleship is set in the light of the cross and resurrection. Understanding of discipleship and understanding of the death of Jesus go hand in hand.

(a) In the first section (8.27–9.29) Peter confesses that Jesus is the Messiah (8.27–30); Jesus explains that his way is the way of suffering, rejection and death (8.31–33). At this point the discussion moves to discipleship. Jesus summons the crowd and the disciples to take up their crosses, deny themselves and come after him (8.34). The contrast of disciples and crowd is not that of leaders of the church and lay people, but of the Christian community and the unevangelised mass outside it. To the crowd outside the call of Jesus is a challenge to begin to follow him. It is equally a challenge to those inside for no one ever gets beyond the stage of learning that discipleship and the cross go together. The gospel on many occasions shows disciples receiving private instruction from Jesus; this could lead members of the community to think that there is some special esoteric or mystical teaching for them to which others have no access. That is not so; disciples are taught exactly the same as the crowd is taught; all understanding of discipleship begins with the cross and it never moves to any other point of orientation. In that respect the teaching here is similar to that of 1 Cor chaps 1, 2; the Corinthians would like to be introduced to a higher wisdom on which they could pride themselves; Paul says that there is no wisdom higher than that of the cross.

Earlier we saw how the blindness of Peter and the disciples was symbolised in the blindness of the man who was healed in two stages.[175] Peter understands that Jesus is important, but does not understand the need for his death. Disciples are in danger of following Jesus but not perceiving that in following him they also must go the way of the cross. They have half sight; they are taught so that they may see more fully. At this point the teaching concentrates on what the cross means for the believer in relation to himself. We pick on three elements (all drawn from 8.34) out of a rich hoard of material.

(i) There is a call to follow or come after Jesus.[176] The disciple is attached to a person. The Jewish rabbi had disciples. He instructed them in the Law; he did not attempt to fix their loyalty on himself but on the Law; thus it was quite proper for a disciple to move from one rabbi to another if he thought the second rabbi could give him better training, for he was not seeking to serve the rabbi but the Law. In the Greek world we find a similar idea in the schools of philosophers, with the possible exception of the Pythagoreans who had a mystical relation to their assumed founder. The philosopher did not seek to attach his pupil to himself but rather to lead him to an understanding of the truth which stood over them both. It is true that both disciples of rabbis and pupils of philosophers often developed a passionate loyalty to their teachers but this was not the desired purpose of their teachers in instructing them. For Mark the disciple is one who obeys the will of God and accomplishes this

[175] Pp. 62, 67f.

[176] On the nature of the call to discipleship made by the historical Jesus see M. Hengel, *The Charismatic Leader and His Followers* (SNTW 1, ET by J.C. Greig), Edinburgh, 1981.

through a personal following of Jesus. While the pupil of the rabbi eventually became a rabbi and the pupil of the philosopher hoped to become a philosopher in his own right, there is no idea in Mark that followers of Jesus become Christs in their own right or in any way take over the place of Jesus. Disciples are always followers attached to Jesus and seek to attach other disciples whom they may win not to themselves but to Jesus. The nature of this attachment will become clearer as we proceed.

(ii) Disciples are called to take up their crosses. In the ancient world the cross was a terrifying means of execution and many of Mark's readers must have seen crucifixions. They could take the reference literally and realise it might be their fate. Yet the element of metaphor was also already beginning to enter the use of the word. While many of Mark's readers might be persecuted and killed few of them would probably be crucified; in the persecutions under Nero crucifixion had not been the usual means of death; 9.1 implies that Mark expects that some Christians will still be alive when Jesus returns. The call to the cross does not then necessarily entail a literal crucifixion but always involves a continual dying which the disciple must take to himself. In common speech we often refer to a cross being laid on someone; in Mark crosses are not laid on people; people take them up and do so voluntarily. To take the cross is to take an active step in the direction of suffering and endurance. The cross is not something thrust on disciples; it does not represent difficult sets of circumstances which they cannot evade; it means that they move forward of their own free will into such difficult situations.

(iii) Disciples are called to deny themselves. Often this is taken to mean that they should deny things to themselves; Hitler denied himself alcohol and tobacco to preserve his throat so that he could address the German people more effectively. But Jesus does not call disciples to deny things to themselves but to deny themselves: whatever they take themselves to be at their deepest level, that must be denied. We can associate with these words those of the next verse (v.35: 'whoever would save his live will lose it; whoever loses his life will save it'). 'Life' here is not just physical life, as if it were only through martyrdom that a person could be saved; nor does it indicate an immortal soul as if the disciple's object were to save some eternal and spiritual inner spark of life. It signifies life at its deepest personal and concrete level. Those who are interested in themselves, even at the deepest, most personal and most religious level will lose themselves; those who forget themselves or deny themselves at those very deep levels will save themselves. But neither self-denial nor self-forgetfulness are human possibilities;

we always hang onto ourselves at the very deepest level. We need some point outside ourselves so that by working from it we can get ourselves out of ourselves. In summarising v.35 above some words were deliberately omitted; the full text runs, 'Whoever loses his life for my sake and the gospel's will save it'. If believers are to deny or lose themselves, they can only achieve this through the dedication of themselves to Jesus and the gospel. Here we can again see, for Mark, the personal attachment of the believer to Jesus. Jesus is much more than another believer or ideal man; he is a saviour.

It is probably important to point out here the distinction between Mark's view of discipleship and discipleship as imitation of Jesus. Taking up of the cross may seem simply a matter of imitation: the believer must adopt the same basic attitude towards suffering as did Jesus himself. But if Mark meant imitation he would have written v.35 differently and put it not as 'whoever loses his life for my sake' but as 'whoever loses his life as I have done will save it'. While the concept of imitation is not absent from Mark's idea of discipleship the idea he puts forwards is much more profound.

There are two further incidents in this section before we reach the second prediction and second section; we have already partly looked at both. In the first, the transfiguration, the centre is the call to disciples to listen to God's beloved son Jesus. In the context of the Gospel Jesus has just spoken profound words about discipleship; God therefore tells the disciples to listen to his teaching. If in the tradition the transfiguration followed after 8.27–33 (the 'after six days' of 9.2 suggests it followed some incident) then 8.34–38 is the centre of a Markan sandwich and should be understood in the light of its two outer portions: the prediction of Jesus' death and the transfiguration. The second incident is that of the boy who was brought to Jesus' disciples by his father so that they should exorcise him; they failed; later Jesus succeeded; the story ends with Jesus instructing the disciples privately; if they wish to exorcise then they must pray. This long story of failure on the part of the disciples and success on the part of Jesus is thus directed towards instruction in discipleship; Mark has inserted it into his Gospel not because it records another miracle but because it tells disciples how they can be better disciples.

(b) The second prediction, 9.30–32, is also followed almost directly by a discussion of discipleship (9.33–10.31), in which disciples are forced to look beyond themselves to their relations with other disciples. Despite Jesus' continual emphasis on the need for suffering the disciples while they have been following him 'on the way' have been discussing among themselves which of them was the greatest. A strong contrast is thus drawn between what he does and their principal concern. When Jesus learns of their discussion he sets a child in their midst (9.33–37). He does not say to them 'You ought to be simple and innocent like children' or 'You ought to think as little of greatness as children do', but 'Whoever receives one such child in my name receives me'. The lesson is not one about imitating children but about receiving children. This probably seems quite strange to us in our child-oriented world. In the ancient world the child was unimportant. Both in the Greek and the Jewish world the ideal was the mature adult; to realise the truth of this we have only to look at Greek statues or to remember that the Jewish boy did not really count as a person until he became a child of the law. Even until quite recently artists depicted children who were thought to be important with adult features. To be contrasted is the way in which children are used today in advertisements in order to attract custom for the advertised product. True greatness consists in receiving the unimportant such as the child in antiquity. Greatness is not realised in the accomplishment of mighty or inspiring tasks and duties, but in reception of and care for the under-privileged of society. Note, before we pass on, how central Jesus is again to the story 'Whoever receives one such child in *my* name receives me'; and once again he is not shown as one to be imitated.

In the next incident (9.38–40) John complains that the disciples have seen a man using the name of Jesus to exorcise and says they stopped him because he was not one of them. Jesus rebukes them and tells them that they ought not to have done so but should have associated him with themselves. The disciples would like to draw the lines of the Christian community and determine who is in it and who is not. This is always a temptation but Jesus does not work from formal definitions of what constitutes a disciple but from the way in which he sees people behaving; if this man is casting out demons using Jesus' name he cannot be wholly opposed to Jesus. The disciples however think of themselves as 'the great ones' and define the boundaries of the Christian fellowship so as to include only themselves. Those who are truly great are always ready to receive others. The incident is generalised in v.41, 'For truly, I say to you, whoever gives you a cup of water to drink because you bear the name of Christ, will by no means lose his reward'. This is a strange verse. The person who offers a cup of water to a disciple because the disciple is a disciple must surely think highly of Christ, that is, be a Christian or on the way to becoming one. Such a person must be accepted and not harshly treated. If harshly treated and made to stumble then a dire fate will overtake the disciple who has done this: 'Whoever causes one of these little ones who believe in me to sin it would be better for him if a great millstone were hung round his neck and he were thrown into the sea' (v.42).

We can quickly skip over the rest of this section. From the danger of making someone stumble the teaching moves on to the danger of stumbling oneself through some obstacle in one's own existence (vv.43–8). Three areas of discipleship are then taken up: marriage, the family, wealth. In each case Mark generalises teaching which had existed prior to him.

(c) This brings us to the third section of the journey to Jerusalem (10.32–45) and the third prediction (10.32–34); this is again followed by a discussion of the nature of greatness. James and John come to Jesus asking for the chief seats in his kingdom when it is established. They are told that such seats are not in Jesus' gift. The remaining disciples complain. Jesus tells them that greatness consists in service: 'Whoever would be great among you must be your servant, and whoever would be first among you must be slave of all' (10.43–4). Although this is often taken to be a discussion of the way in which authority should be exercised it is in reality a radical denial of any exercise of authority. It is not argued that those who rule should do so humbly in a spirit of service. The contrast is made rather between authority, good or bad, and service. The Christian will be a servant and a slave. Two words, service and slavery, are picked from the secular sphere to describe discipleship. The first of these, service or ministry, was later used by Paul and the early church to describe the activity of those holding positions of preeminence or authority within the church; in Mark on Jesus' lips it refers to service of a personal nature freely offered to others. The disciple is to be one who continually offers such personal service.

Finally discipleship is brought back into a relationship to Jesus. 'For the Son of man came not to be served but to serve, and to give his life as a ransom for many' (10.45). The first half of that verse might suggest that the disciple and his Master were carrying through the same task, but the second half makes absolute the distinction between Master and servant. The servant is never summoned to give his life as ransom for others in the way the Master has given his. And indeed it is only because the Master has given his life that the servant is able to offer service to others. We note that in the directly following incident (10.46–52) Bartimaeus, his sight restored, is able to go 'on the way' after Jesus. To 'see' as Bartimaeus sees requires a miracle; it is not a simple human accomplishment; it is achieved through Jesus' life as ransom, through his cross and resurrection, on which all discipleship is founded.

(d) At the end of the central section (8.27–10.52) we move directly into the last days of Jesus in Jerusalem (11.1ff.). Attention is focussed almost entirely on him and the disciples naturally slip into the background; there are however two ways in which they feature to which we may draw attention.

(1) The need for watchfulness is stressed twice. In the Gethsemane incident (14.32–42) the disciples fall asleep and fail to be watchful. It is possible that Mark has developed a single reference to their sleep into a threefold; in any case he seems to have added v.38, 'Watch and pray that you may not enter into temptation; the spirit indeed is willing, but the flesh is weak', and the latter part of v.40 'for their eyes were very heavy; and they did not know what to answer him'. In v.40 we meet again the theme of sight and blindness. The eyes of the disciples are heavy; they are not totally blind but have difficulty in seeing. If they are to stay awake then they need to watch and pray. Verse 38, 'the spirit is willing', may contain a reference to the Holy Spirit, with the contrast not between the flesh and the spirit of man, but between man as weak flesh and the Holy Spirit as strong. Through prayer the Christian receives this strong Spirit and so is able to stand. The second reference to watchfulness comes at the end of the Little Apocalypse. This closes with the short parable (13.34–7) of the man who has gone on a journey and left his servants to take care of his property and watch for his return. We can clearly detect here the eschatological expectation of the early Christians who believe the Messiah will return speedily. They do not know when and therefore must be alert so that he does not come and catch them unprepared. This watchfulness may seem unrelated to that which is advocated in Gethsemane and unrelated to the wider theme of discipleship exercised in suffering. Mark's community, however, would have seen all their suffering as eschatologically orientated. Disciples must not allow their suffering to make them less alert.

(2) In Gethsemane the disciples are told how to endure: through prayer. At the cross itself they fail. Are they then lost? What of those from Mark's community who fail in trial or persecution? This is answered with an example of restoration. When Jesus is arrested the disciples flee; Peter denies him three times. It seems as if there is no hope yet the message which the young man gives at the empty tomb is to go and tell Peter and the disciples that Jesus is risen. Hope is renewed for them. On the other hand the example of Judas shows that restoration is not automatic; Judas is not exluded from the message of 16.7, but Mark's readers must have known, as we know, that before the message could reach him he had taken his own life.

(e) Journeys can be lonely and much of the exhortation to the disciples to deny themselves and take up their crosses may seem to impose upon them a terrible strain. Mark's Gospel itself always implies the presence with the disciple of the risen Lord through his words and actions. But there is also aid for loneliness from another angle: 'on the way' with the disciple there are always other disciples; the disciple is never alone. Since this has come out in much of what we have already said it is only necessary now to allude briefly to it.

The instruction given to the disciples about the nature of true greatness implies their existence in a group; without a group the concept of relative greatness would not exist. The disciples are regularly taught privately in houses or in ships; the house would remind Mark's community of their own houses where daily or weekly services are held.[177] All instruction in the words of the living Jesus is then corporate instruction. House-churches are places of fellowship; the Christian may have been driven out of his own home and lost his biological father or mother or brother or sister, but within the new community he or she has met up with a hundred other fathers and mothers and brothers and sisters (10.28–30). The Christian is never an isolated individual but always a member of a flock whose shepherd is Jesus. The old temple which received God's judgement through Jesus is replaced with a new temple not made with hands, the new community in which God himself dwells, for temples are places where gods dwell. This new community came into existence with the resurrection, being created after three days. It is also the house of prayer for all nations; no one is to be excluded because of race or colour.

There is no trace of a ministry within the community. That is not to say there was no ministry. We do not know to what stage ministry had developed in Rome at the time Mark was writing; he is not interested in it. In so far as he depicts the Twelve as exercising a ministry it is one towards the outside world; they are sent to teach and exorcise; they are not given authority over others within the community. The outward reach of the community moreover is not restricted to their particular official ministry. As we have seen disciples, and this means all disciples, are from the beginning sent to fish. They are instructed to receive children, the unimportant members of society, and take care of them. The outward reach of all disciples is implied in the demand made on the rich man (10.21); disciples should use their wealth for the good of the poor,

[177] See p. 63.

and this cannot be restricted to the poor of the community itself. Jesus goes as their shepherd at their head into Galilee, into the place of preaching. The whole community has been given a mission.

(f) Finally we return to the journey which forms the backbone of the second half of the Gospel. Journeys have goals. People travel because they wish to reach destinations. The theme of pilgrimage and journey has been common in Christianity. The saints travel toward their heavenly abode. Abraham was a traveller. The best known treatment of the travel theme in the New Testament is in Hebrews where the people of God journey towards the heavenly city; nothing endures here; all is transient; but there is an abiding city, and this is their goal.

What then is the goal for Mark? It might be said to be the cross. Disciples are told to take up their crosses; they travel with Jesus to Jerusalem and death. But this would only be the goal in any real sense if martyrdom was envisaged as the end of each pilgrim's life, and we have seen this is not so. Jesus goes to Jerusalem and his death but after his death the tomb is empty; he has gone beyond Jerusalem. His own prediction and that of the young man at the tomb indicate that he has gone to Galilee; the disciples are to follow him. Thus the journey runs through Jerusalem and the cross to the risen Jesus and Galilee, the place of mission. It is wrong to speak of the cross as the goal; it is even wrong to speak of the mission as the goal. These are two modes of existence, one of suffering, one of risen life. At all times Christians are living in both modes. As they go on the way of the cross they suffer but are continually renewed because they are also going on the way of the risen Jesus in Galilee. For Mark the goal might be more adequately described as Jesus himself rather than the cross or even the cross and the resurrection. Jesus is not however a fixed or static goal to whom travellers are always drawing nearer but a dynamic goal who is continually moving ahead of them. The journey on which the disciples go is open-ended, a journey in mission towards the world. It is a journey outwards and beyond, determined in its nature by the cross and the resurrection, but never a limited journey.

Yet for Mark it is not an unlimited journey. Leaving aside all question of the death of believers, the road ends when Christ returns. The journey takes believers on a path of suffering and persecution but also on a path of mission. When mission has been fulfilled and the gospel has been preached to all nations (13.10) then comes the end of all journeying.

CHAPTER XV

MARK'S PURPOSE

It is now time to begin to draw together what we have done and see how far we have got in answering our initial questions.

(1) There is no need to challenge the traditional view that the Gospel was written in Rome.[178]

(2) There does not seem to have been any historical event which was the direct cause of the Gospel. It may be that the death of eye-witnesses, the fall of Jerusalem and the danger of persecution were contributory factors but none was the actual occasion of the Gospel; still less was it the threat of a divine-man christology.

(3) What was Mark's purpose in writing the Gospel? It was not primarily polemical; Mark is not a controversialist, least of all an academic controversialist, but a pastor. Neither was his purpose merely to give information about the life of Jesus; his book certainly provides a large proportion of the information available to us but we have to dig into it with great care in order to unearth it with any accuracy; if his Gospel and the others had not been written we would have been almost devoid of knowledge of the historical Jesus. He supplies information but he uses it to sustain his community. He did not write out of some inner urge to express himself; there have been poets who wrote without thought of those who would read them; Mark always had in mind those for whom he was writing.

If Mark's purpose was pastoral he was not writing a tract for the community to use outside itself. A.E.J. Rawlinson[179] believed Mark, in addition to attempting to meet a natural curiosity about how Christianity began, wrote in order to supply material for evangelists and preachers and for apologists in controversy with Jews and heathen. C.F.D. Moule[180] agrees with Rawlinson but seems to go a little further in suggesting that the Gospel itself may have been written to be used outside the community for evangelical and apologetical purposes. Certainly many of the individual

---

[178] See above pp. 35f.

[179] *The Gospel According to St. Mark* (Westminster Commentaries), London, 1925, pp. xii, xiv, xv.

[180] 'The Intention of the Evangelists' in *New Testament Essays: Studies in Memory of T.W. Manson* (ed. A.J.B. Higgins), Manchester, 1959, pp. 165–179 at p. 167.

pericopae were in use for these purposes before Mark wrote; the suggestion therefore fails to account for the particular form of the Gospel; why did Mark put the material together in the way he did? All we have said about the structure and content of the Gospel would also lead us to reject such an explanation of the Gospel's purpose. We may formulate our objections more precisely: (i) It is not only the crowd who are taught but also the disciples, and as the Markan redaction shows the essential teaching is given to the latter; the disciples are representatives of Mark's community, not of the outside world. (ii) The essential teaching given to them, while it in part concerns God's purposes and the meaning of the Christ-event, relates these to discipleship, that is to the quality of the life of disciples, and not in the first instance to their relationship to the outside world. (iii) While some passages deal with the summons to all disciples to approach the outside world and win the crowd into the community yet the Twelve seem to represent a group of special missionaries appointed by the Church to carry out the main evangelical task; yet the Gospel is written to benefit the whole community and not these special missionaries alone. (iv) The flow of the narrative is such that it moves on from the position of those who have been attracted to Christianity by charismatic wonders and are now in the church to the need for the opening of their eyes to a truer understanding of their faith. The emphasis on the 'blindness' and 'stupidity' of the disciples and of the family of Jesus is inexplicable on the view of Rawlinson and Moule. (v) The account of the arrest, trial and death of Jesus could have been used for evangelistic purposes but as it appears in Mark's Gospel with additions like the account of the Last Supper and the anointing of the head of Jesus it is intended for church use. (vi) While the parable of the sower on its own might be used in missionary activity its interpretation in 4.14–20 deals with the temptations to which Christians are exposed and the need for their steadfastness; the latter is hardly relevant to missionary preaching. (vii) 4.10–12,33f. imply that the Gospel can only be understood by those who are already within the community; if this was intended for outsiders we should expect an invitation, 'Come inside and we shall explain everything to you'. (viii) While there are 'calls' to outsiders to become disciples of Jesus these are not straightforward invitations; to them is linked the invitation to be 'fishers of men', i.e., to participate in missionary work. The primary emphasis lies on this latter invitation and therefore seems to be directed to those who are already within the church. Disciples go apart with Jesus at times from the crowd into 'houses'; but the difference between them and the crowd has already been made clear. Jesus does not take outsiders away by themselves for particular instruction; he continues the instruction of those who are already his. (ix) Although the Old Testament is not used extensively in Mark it is used in such a way that its appeal would only affect those who already know it, and that means Christians, unless we view the Gospel as directed only towards Jews; the latter is highly unlikely. (x) Moule tests the kerygma of the Gospel by the Pauline kerygma and because Mark does not seem to have the same emphases as Paul he denies the kerygmatic nature of Mark; he fails to recognise that there is a variety of kerygmata in the New Testament. (xi) Moule fails to place the Gospel in a living situation in the early church; he suggests an 'evangelistic' situation but the evidence for it is not drawn from the Gospel itself.

J.H. Ropes[181] suggests Mark's purpose was to explain the stumblingblock of the cross and that he does this by giving a historical account which showed Jesus as living a life of love and as wrongly accused and also by arguing that his death could be seen as the fulfilment of a divine plan. So much of the Gospel (e.g., the parables of chap 4, the miracles, the teaching on discipleship) is not related to these ends that it becomes impossible to accept this solution.

Mark then writes as a pastor for his community which he is concerned to deepen in its understanding of the Gospel. The gospel is not something to be proclaimed to outsiders alone; the rigid distinction sometimes drawn between missionary preaching to the world and teaching within the church would not have been acceptable to Mark. The gospel as it is proclaimed still speaks to the community and should change the way in which its members live.

Other pastoral purposes are possible and recently Standaert[182] has suggested, though somewhat tentatively, that the Gospel was designed for reading in the church at Rome during the pascal vigil; this would be followed on Easter morning with the baptism of new converts. He argues:

(1) The Gospel has a special interest in baptism. (a) The discussion of the nature of discipleship, one of the most prominent themes in the Gospel, is very relevant to new converts.[183] Yet the exhortation to discipleship cannot end for catechumens with their baptism; it is a theme to which their pastors must continually recur, even when speaking to those who have been baptised many years.

---

[181] *The Synoptic Gospels,* Oxford, 1960, p. 10.
[182] Op. cit. (as n. 11), *passim.*
[183] Op. cit., pp. 325, 498–502.

(b) There are a number of passages which deal directly with the meaning of baptism for Christians, e.g. 14.51f.; 10.38.[184] (c) Mark is a drama and says in its own way what Rom 6.1–11 says in its: we follow Christ to his death so that we may follow him in his glory.[185] (d) According to the principles of dramatic and rhetorical composition the prologue and the epilogue of a book are the most important sections for understanding it;[186] the prologue features the general baptism carried out by John the Baptizer and his special baptism of Jesus; the epilogue (16.1–8) takes place at dawn when baptism would be held following the pascal vigil; the young man of 16.5 is related to baptism. But we may ask whether the baptisms of John the Baptizer and in particular his baptism of Jesus could appear at any point other than at the beginning of the book? Furthermore any solution to the problem of the references to the young men in 14.51f. and 16.5 must be at best very tentative.[187] More importantly we have no knowledge of the baptismal practice in the church at Rome in the time of Mark; we do not know if there was a catechetical period before baptism and if candidates were held back until Easter morning before being baptized; nothing elsewhere in the New Testament suggests this practice; indeed if Acts is to be believed and if it reflects in part the practice of Luke's own time which is later than Mark's, then this did not happen; baptism took place directly after conversion. Standaert provides some evidence from second and third century material but this is not of much help, especially as some of it is drawn from heretical sources.[188]

(2) The context of the Gospel is pascal. Many pascal themes are present: (a) Mark is aware of and depends on the 'poem of the four nights';[189] one of the nights is connected to the Exodus and another to the Passover in relation to which the Aqedah Isaac is an important theme, as it is in the Gospel.[190] (b) There are many reminiscences of the Exodus in the prologue,[191] e.g. John the Baptizer preaches in the wilderness, Jesus spends forty days in the wilderness. (c) Jesus is the new Moses.[192] John the Baptizer is the messenger who precedes the new Moses, the dove indicates Jesus as

[184] Op. cit., pp. 153–168, 503.
[185] Op. cit., pp. 502–4.
[186] Op. cit., pp. 504–512.
[187] See above pp. 26f.
[188] Op. cit., pp. 527–537.
[189] Cf. R. le Déaut, *La Nuit Pascale* (Anal. Bib. 22), Rome, 1963.
[190] See above pp. 81f.
[191] Standaert, as n. 11, pp. 547–554.
[192] Op. cit., pp. 550, 554–566.

the new Moses. The words of the Divine voice in 1.11 refer to the Isaianic servant and imply that Jesus is the new Moses. Jesus was tempted for forty days as Moses was forty years in the wilderness. Jesus is *the* prophet who is the new Moses[193] of 6.16; Moses appears beside Jesus in the transfiguration (9.2–8) and the words 'Hear him' come from Deut 15.18. Yet the order of the names of Moses and Elijah is inverted so that Elijah comes first and is featured in the following discussion (vv.9–13) whereas Moses is forgotten. (d) The transfiguration can be linked to the fourth night of the 'poem of the four nights'.[194] (e) The epilogue by its position and content clearly has pascal connections; but could the book end with any other connections? Much of what Standaert suggests is forced and fanciful. There is hardly a book in the New Testament which has not got many pascal references. The best evidence is supplied from the 'poem of the four nights' but even this does not take us very far.

(3) The early church had pascal vigils and there are references to these in Mark in the Gethsemane incident (14.32–42) and in the conclusion to the Little Apocalypse (13.32–7); the latter passage however is related to the parousia and not to Easter; the former can be related easily to the general life of the believer. The evidence for a pascal vigil comes at earliest from the second century; it is impossible to find it in the New Testament. Standaert points to the fact that sometimes people watch and pray at night (Acts 16.9,25; 12.1ff.); it is statistically obvious that they should pray sometimes at night for night occupies twelve of the twenty four hours of a day and there is not much else to be done at night apart from sleeping but to pray, especially when as in those days artificial light was a luxury. Christians also pray in the day-time (Acts 9.11f.; 10.9,30; 20.36; 20.17). There is certainly a late night meeting in Acts 20.7–16 which takes place at the time of Easter (cf. 20.6) but Luke presents this as a service and not as a vigil.

(4) Some Jewish literature was composed for use at festivals, e.g., Esther, Judith[195], and the Jews may have had Passover vigils. This does not prove that Mark was written for a pascal vigil.

(5) Certain other New Testament writings are pascal and Standaert indicates in particular 1 Peter;[196] we very much doubt if this is the purpose and context of that letter.[197]

[193] Op. cit., pp. 571–3.
[194] Op. cit., pp. 574f.
[195] Op. cit., p. 603.
[196] Op. cit., pp. 604f.
[197] Cf. Best, *1 Peter* (New Century Bible), London, 1971, pp. 21ff. and the literature cited there. See more recently, L. Goppelt, *Der erste Petrusbrief* (KEK), Göttingen, 1978, pp. 38–40.

Standaert only puts forward his proposal as a suggestion. We cannot feel that he has given sufficient evidence to require its acceptance. In addition he leaves unanswered the question why Mark should have written the particular form of document which he has written. Why is this form of writing most suitable to a vigil? Large sections have no particular relevance.

R.P. Martin[198] suggests a very different pastoral purpose. He argues that there was a latent ambiguity in Paul's presentation of the cross which later led to emphasis being placed on Christ as a heavenly figure remote from empirical history and out of touch with earthly reality; this ended in a gnostic version of Christianity in the second century. Mark saw the danger and wrote his Gospel to counter it. He put together just those individual sections of the pre-canonical tradition which emphasise the paradox of Jesus' earthly life in which suffering and vindication form a two-beat rhythm.[199] His christology is that of a teacher who has caught the essence of Paul's thought, yet expressed it by the use of language and terminology to which Paul had no access (the Jesus-tradition) and did so in order to compensate for what he believed to be a serious distortion of his master's thought as apostle par excellence.

At the same time he attempted to show that the disciples' way must also be one of suffering which would end in glory. 'In sum, the evangelist is offering a dramatization in the life of Jesus, by a selective use of the materials at his disposal and by his innovative joining of a Jesus-tradition and a Passion narrative, of the twin elements which made up the Pauline preaching. These are the humiliation and enthronement of the church's Lord.'[200]

Leaving aside the question whether Mark was a disciple of Paul, which seems to be implicit in Martin's position, but is unprovable, there are more serious objections. The tradition about Jesus which Mark used was already known to his community; it may not have been known to some of the Pauline communities, e.g. Corinth, but Mark was not writing for Corinth. In order to emphasise the historical reality of Jesus there was no need for him to write a gospel. There is nothing in the Gospel as it exists to suggest that he was reminding them of something that they did not know; were he emphasising the historical reality of Jesus as a new idea, then his approach would have been different. The movement of the Gospel is towards the cross and resurrection; the events in Jesus' life are

---

[198] As n. 39, pp. 156–162.

[199] Cf. W. Luz, 'Das Geheimnismotiv und die markinische Christologie', *ZNW* 56 (1965) 9–30.

[200] Martin, as n. 39, p. 161.

seen in the light of the cross and resurrection; Martin's theory requires that the cross and the resurrection be seen in the light of the historical events. Finally, if Martin is correct we must doubt whether Mark has written the right kind of book to meet the danger he forsaw; the miracles are not set aside and are certainly not treated in such a way as to bring out an anti-docetic or anti-enthusiastic trend; much other material, e.g. the parables, is unrelated to the alleged main purpose.

Pastoral activity can have many different orientations, just as the Gospel might have been written for the internal consumption of the community for various reasons. In saying that Mark wrote as a pastor we of course exclude the idea that he wrote primarily to give information about Jesus or to defend his community from christological heresy. He sought, in the very widest sense, to build them up in the faith.

CHAPTER XVI

THE CEMENT OF THE GOSPEL

(4) What is the glue or cement which holds the material together? Is it something imposed arbitrarily on the material from outside or does it inhere in the material? How are the various pericopae organised into a unity? It might be answered that the events follow one another in the historical order in which they happened in the life of Jesus. Obviously this must be true of some of them but as we have seen most already lacked temporal and geographical details by the time Mark came to use them. He would not have known their chronological order and would have had no means of finding it out. What principle did he then use when he put them together? From time to time elaborate theories have been evolved to account for the order in which the material appears. A.M. Farrer[201] suggested a scheme based on numerology in relation to the miracles; John Bowman[202] thought that the Gospel was related to the Passover Liturgy; Philip Carrington[203] believed that the order of the material was dictated by the liturgical needs of the church. In this last case it was clearly something outside the material which was used to cement it together. None of these views has stood up to examination. With superficially more justification C.H. Dodd[204] suggested that a summary of the life of Jesus was current in the early church and that this provided the structural backbone for the Gospel. It is doubtful if such a summary ever existed, but, even if it did and Mark possessed it, it was so brief that he would still have been in grave doubt where to place by far the greater part of the material; it would not have told him the relative positioning of the miracles to one another or the positioning of the parables in relation to the miracles, or the positioning of much of the teaching on discipleship in respect of both miracles and parables.[205] The alleged summary is not then the cement of the Gospel.

---

[201] *A Study in St. Mark,* Westminster, 1951.

[202] *The Gospel of Mark: The New Christian Jewish Passover Haggadah,* Leiden, 1965.

[203] *The Primitive Christian Calendar: A Study in the Making of the Markan Gospel,* Cambridge, 1952. See now, M.D. Goulder, *The Evangelists' Calendar,* London, 1978, pp. 241ff.

[204] 'The Framework of the Gospel Narratives' in his *New Testament Studies,* Manchester, 1953, pp. 1–11.

[205] For criticism of Dodd's theory see D.E. Nineham, 'The Order of Events in St. Mark's Gospel – an Examination of Dr. Dodd's Hypothesis', in *Studies in the Gospels* (ed. Nineham), Oxford, 1955, pp. 223–239; F.C. Grant, *The Earliest Gospel,* New York and Nashville, 1943, pp. 46ff.

Yet on the other hand Mark did not have a wholly free hand in the way the material could be put together. The Last Supper had to be set in the immediate context of Jesus' death; the baptism needed to be inserted near the beginning of the story. Some groups of material had already been joined together prior to Mark: 1.20–39 was probably an existing unit suggesting what a day in the life of Jesus was like; the parables of 4.1–34 were united to one another before Mark took them over; he may have used an existing catena of miracle stories in 4.35ff.; the pericopae about divorce, children and wealth were probably an existing unit. A great deal of work has been done on the nature of the pre-Markan form of the passion story, but no consensus has yet emerged as to its outline;[206] almost certainly the story had some structure prior to Mark; to a greater or less extent he has added to this structure. However, even when we take all this into account we are no nearer an answer to the question of Mark's organising principle.

Standaert[207] argues that Mark is held together by the accepted conventions of rhetoric and drama. The Gospel is therefore not *Kleinliteratur.* That Mark's style is not elegant and does not correspond to these conventions is only because he has made it to fit the recipients, a practice recognised in the ancient world.[208] Whether Mark himself was educated in Palestine or in Rome his education almost certainly included instruction in these conventions.

Standaert outlines the sketch of the elementary structure of a discourse, *exordium, narratio, probatio, refutatio, conclusio,* and suggests that Mark contains these divisions in the same order: 1.1–13; 1.14–6.13; 6.14–10.52; 11.1–15.47; 16.1–8.[209] Standaert also points to the concentric composition of individual sections and sub-sections so that there is a careful balancing of one paragraph or sentence against another.[210] 8.27–9.13 provides a good example of this concentric composition with 8.27–30 balancing 9.11–13 and 8.31–33 balancing 9.2–10, and 8.34–9.1 remaining as the centre of the passage. Standaert also argues that between the main divisions there are traditional passages which carry on the argument.

He may be supported generally by the argument that if there was anywhere in the ancient world where the canons of rhetoric might have been followed it would be the city of Rome; here a 'relatively sophisticated' rhetorical level might be expected. George Kennedy

---

[206] Cf. above n. 75.
[207] Op. cit. (as n. 11), *passim.*
[208] Op. cit., p. 465.
[209] Op. cit., pp. 42f.
[210] Op. cit., pp. 174ff.

in discussion at the San Antonio colloquium on the Gospels said 'Some knowledge of rhetorical techniques and conventions inevitably would have filtered down to the lower levels of society and would have coloured the expectations, perhaps unconsciously, of those who listened to early Christian preachers or read early Christian literature.'[211] The early Christian community would have contained a number of 'God-fearers' who would have had some education.

Standaert also holds that Mark followed the conventions of dramatic writing though, as he admits, our knowledge of contemporary drama and the rules for its composition is fragmentary.[212] Good examples of Mark's dramatic approach are provided by the accounts of the death of John the Baptist and the passion of Jesus. As in a dramatic composition there is a prologue in which John the Baptizer may be said to serve as the 'messenger' *(aggelos)*; similarly in the prologue the young man at the tomb functions as the 'messenger', or the *deus ex machina.* Again the transitional sections are important in taking us from one part of the drama to another.

We may ask whether Standaert does not confuse the natural way in which the good teller of a tale expresses his material with the art of writing a drama. Many people who have had no instruction in dramatic composition may yet have a natural flair for storytelling[213] so that as they tell the story they build up the tension in their hearers.

> The tribal Story Teller is a deliberate artist. Long before 'literature' was invented he charmed, as in simple communities he still charms the wide-eyed circle about the camp-fire or beneath the village tree.[214]

In the absence of detailed knowledge of contemporary drama it is hard to argue for much more than this in the case of Mark.

There are also other minor points more directly concerned with dramatic structure. In the epilogue it would have been more in accordance with dramatic convention if Mark had introduced an actual divine messenger rather than a young man and if he was consciously writing in imitation of dramas there seems no reason why he should not have done so (cf. Matt 28.2,3). However much

---

[211] See Walker (as n. 6), p. 184.

[212] Op. cit., p. 65.

[213] See below pp. 128ff. for the natural dramatic elements in the Gospel.

[214] J.H.K. Thomson, *The Art of the Logos,* London, 1935, quoted in T. Boman, op. cit. (see n. 8), p. 242, n. 32.

more important than any such minor issue is a consideration of the control which Mark as dramatist was able to exercise over his material. In historical drama, and we need not consider drama which is purely fictional, the writer while remaining loyal to the main lines of what has come to him in history will feel himself free in what he writes to improvise the words and actions of speakers and the relation of actors to one another. Did Mark write incidents to fit particular points of the drama he was composing? Did he have a limited number of incidents at his disposal which he simply shuffled around until he found the best place for each in the development of his drama? Did he have a large number of incidents from the tradition from which he was able to select a few so that he could the more easily fulfil his purposes? Standaert does not consider any of these questions.[215]

When we examine some of the examples (e.g. 8.27–9.13) of concentric composition which Standaert provides doubts arise as to Mark's competency in this matter. It would have been a simple matter in 8.28 for Mark to have changed 'one of the prophets' to 'the prophet' indicating Moses who appears later (9.4) in this set of pericopae; the Divine voice in the transfiguration (9.7) balances Peter's confession in 8.29 yet this does not fit in with Standaert's concentric composition; it is probable that the original account of the transfiguration referred only to Peter and that Mark added James and John; the balance would have been better, supposing he had intended a balance, if he had inserted a reference to all the disciples. To argue that Mark did not deliberately create a concentric composition here is not to say that the material has not been arranged by Mark; in the preceding tradition the account of the transfiguration was probably related to 8.27–30 and possibly also 8.31–33; Mark inserted 8.34–9.1, and 8.31–33 if it was not already attached to 8.34–9.1.

That Mark can be outlined in accordance with the conventions of rhetoric does not prove that his gospel was designed to follow those conventions. It is quite easy to divide Ruth into the five standard categories of *exordium* etc.: 1.1–5; 1.6–2.23; 3.1–18; 4.1–12; 4.13–22. No one would suggest that its author was aware of the conventions of rhetoric. It is not quite as clear as Standaert suggests that Mark lowered his style to that of the uneducated recipients of his writing; his style can be described as nothing other than 'heavy'.[216] Its infelicities can be explained more easily on the

---

[215] On Mark's control over his material see below pp. 107f., 112–4, 128ff.

[216] Cf. N. Turner in J.H. Moulton, *A Grammar of New Testament Greek,* Vol 4, Edinburgh, 1976, pp. 11–30.

supposition that this is the normal style of a partly educated man. If, as Standaert supposes,[217] Mark adapted his language to suit his readers would he not also have adapted the larger element of style? Kennedy, whom we quoted earlier, also remarks[218] that 'the Gospels do not exhibit a conscious artifice of style designed for rhetorical effect'. The rhetorical conventions were only taught at the third and highest level of education.[219] Would Mark have expected his hearers to pick out the meaning of what he was writing if they did not know the accepted conventions? If they could not do this of what help would it be to them that the writing was framed in this way? How would they have understood his meaning better? Lastly, even granted that Mark adopted the rhetorical conventions, this does not answer the question why he wrote in the form he did. Why did he not write a more genuine discourse giving the teaching of Jesus or a more genuine drama playing out what happened to Jesus? What is the relation of the rhetorical conventions to the theological thought which Mark is attempting to express? Which is really in control? Standaert does not answer these questions.[220]

Apart from Standaert there has been an increasing number of attempts to see Mark's composition as governed by the rhetorical conventions. Many examples might be given; one will suffice. Joanna Dewey[221] has argued strongly for concentric parallelism in some parts of Mark. Her work is careful and restrained; she wishes neither to exclude other methods of study nor to claim that all of the Gospel has been written in this way; she also sees a forward movement within the material as well as a concentric. She has examined 2.1–3.6 in great detail and argued for concentric parallelism as an aid to its explanation. As clues to concentric patterns she posits 'multiple *congruent* parallelisms of content, form-critical classification, structure, and word repetition (hook words)'.[222] She finds all these present in Mark 2.1–3.6.

It is impossible to summarise her long and detailed discussion; she has certainly made out a good case. Many details may however

---

[217] See n. 11, p. 465.

[218] Art. cit. in Walker (see n. 6), p. 185.

[219] Cf. H.-I. Marrou, *Histoire de l'education dans l'antiquité,* Paris, 1948, pp. 200ff., 359ff.; A.J. Malherbe, *Social Aspects of Early Christianity,* Baton Rouge and London, 1977, pp. 29ff.; M.P. Nilsson, *Die hellenistische Schule,* München, 1955.

[220] J.I.H. McDonald, *Kerygma and Didache* (SNTS Monograph Series 37) Cambridge, 1980, pp. 63f., argues that the thematic homily 'provided the framework for a new *Gattung,* the written Gospel'. He supplies no real discussion of, or justification for this hypothesis.

[221] *Markan Public Debate* (SBL Dissertation Series 48) Chico, Calif., 1980.

[222] Op. cit., p. 168.

be questioned. When she notes[223] that 2.1 and 3.1 both use the verb *eiserchomai* with the preposition *eis* and the adverb *palin* she fails to note that Mark regularly uses the verb plus preposition when introducing incidents (cf. 1.21,45; 2.1,26; 3.1; 7.17,24; 9.28; 11.11,15) and the adverb is one of Mark's favourite words. The parallelism between 2.1 and 3.1 is therefore much less significant than she suggests. When she argues that Mark introduces Jesus as the son of man in 2.10 and 2.28 so that when further reference is made to the son of man from 8.31 onwards readers will know that Jesus is intended[224] she forgets that Mark is not a book written for outsiders who will approach it from a position of ignorance, but a book written for insiders who already have in their minds the equation 'Jesus is the son of man'.[225] An early preparatory statement of this equation was therefore unnecessary. In the course of her work she is naturally compelled to argue, against prevailing scholarly opinion, that 2.1–3.6 was not a pre-Markan complex.[226]

With a little ingenuity it is possible to see other concentric structures which are probably not deliberately intended. One which could be alleged to exist and which would interfere with her proposal (this is the reason for its present suggestion!) is 1.40–2.17. This consists of three incidents (1.40–45; 2.1–12; 2.13–17) all of which are related to sin. Leprosy is a type of sin; a leper is cleansed just as a sinner is cleansed.[227] 1.40–45 begins with a cleansing = forgiveness of a sinner and ends with his proclamation of the Gospel. 2.13–17 begins with the reception of a sinner (Levi) and ends with his proclamation of the Gospel in that he throws a party to which he invites tax collectors and sinners. Both lepers and the tax collectors were outcasts from Israelite society and in both cases Jesus links himself closely with them. The central section 2.1–12 again clearly brings out the theme of sin and shows that Jesus has the authority to forgive it. Not all the parallelism may be perfect here but then as Dewey allows 'Ancient authors on rhetoric or literary criticism may be cited either praising the lack of perfect balance or condemning too perfect balance'.[228] (This is a clear 'heads I win, tails you lose' argument.)

Two final points may be made. If Mark was written to be listened to and not just to be read in the study, would the concentric parallelism be as easily detected by an original hearer as Dewey

---

[223] Op. cit., p. 101.
[224] Op. cit., p. 125; cf. p. 192.
[225] Op. cit., p. 125.
[226] Op. cit., pp. 52–55, 181ff.; her view is slightly modified on p. 193.
[227] See my *The Temptation and the Passion,* (as n. 103), pp. 106f.
[228] Op. cit., p. 123.

suggests? If it was not easy to detect, did Mark really intend it? It is impossible to re-iterate too often that there are great dangers in studying Mark as a written document and forgetting it was designed to be heard. Certain structures may also be quite natural to certain minds and therefore not have any necessary theological or exegetical significance. My students tell me that it is common for me to list a number of issues in a subject and then to say 'Let us take these in reverse order'; this creates a chiastic structure, but it seems to emerge from the way my mind is made rather than from any deliberate literary plan. It would not be surprising then to find in Mark elements of concentric parallelism without supposing that they are deeply significant for his thought, or that they reveal much about his meaning. Finally we should keep in mind the wise words of A.N. Wilder:

> The classical writers stood above their material as artists portraying their subjects for the book-trade, while our evangelists are devoutly ordering for local believers the testimonies provided for them by tradition not as biography but as the cult story of faith.[229]

It would be wrong to think of Mark entering his study and saying to himself 'Now I must write a Gospel' or 'Now I must write the story down for people to read and study in solitude'. The story he later wrote down he may have already told several times orally and then been asked by the leaders of the church to put it on paper or he may himself have thought of doing so. That Mark had told the story several times before he wrote it down is not an improbable assumption. Communities which preserve and pass on oral tradition normally do so through particular individuals who possess some talent for the task. A story teller who cannot string his material together in such a way that he attracts and holds the attention of his hearers is soon not listened to at all. Thus we should expect that Mark was a known reciter of the oral tradition in his community.[230] We should also expect that his talents were those of someone accustomed to handle oral material effectively; when he wrote his material down it would thus tend to follow the modes of oral recitation rather than those of written composition. Anyone who tells anecdotes knows he varies them each time he tells them; not every oral recitation of a story would be the same as every other;[231] each would show variation and in a certain sense would be

---

[229] *Early Christian Rhetoric: The Language of the Gospel,* London, 1964, p. 39; cf. p. 24.

[230] To suppose with Boman (as n. 8), pp. 44ff. that the term *hupēretai* refers to such people formalizes the position too much.

[231] Cf. A.B. Lord, as n. 29, pp. 63, 109ff.

a fresh creation, an original,[232] for there would have been no fixed model to follow. If Mark had narrated the story orally before he wrote it down the written form would also have been slightly different. The very fact of the comparative slowness of written composition in comparison with oral recitation would lead to modification, probably the disappearance of some of the more ornate and vivid detail. If it was dictated, and we cannot affirm it was not, there would again be omission of detail, though the pauses between clauses in the dictation would give Mark more time to think about what he was going to say next. It is difficult to see how this would affect what he did in other ways. It certainly does not imply that he would necessarily use the methods of the rhetoricians. Attempts to discover such rhetorical planning by no means always agree; like those of the somewhat different approaches of Farrer and Carrington, who also envisaged rigid planning, they lie more often in the eye of the beholder than in the mind of Mark. We must allow however that even if Mark had not attended a school where rhetoric was taught, and it is most unlikely that he had, some of the broader principles of composition would have percolated down from these schools to the general public.[233] These broader principles are in a way natural to careful composers of stories and would be quickly assimilated by a lively mind; compare how some students seem to have a natural ability to pick up the correct way to answer examination questions and write essays.

Criticism of attempts at rhetorical criticism of Mark should not then be taken to suggest that he did not arrange his material. An important example of how he did this is seen in the way Jesus does not reach Jerusalem until the last week of his life. There is strong evidence to show he was there at other times. According to the Fourth Gospel Jesus visited Jerusalem several times; the cry over Jerusalem (Mt 23.37ff.; Lk 13.34ff.) would imply his knowledge of the life of the city; Jesus was probably known to the man who lent him the donkey for his entry (Mk 11.2ff.); he was at home in the house of Simon the leper as if he had visited there before (14.3–9); he is able to use a friend's house for the Last Supper (14.12–16); he taught often in the temple (14.49); Joseph of Arimathea is a member of the Sanhedrin and has at his disposal a tomb in which Jesus is laid (15.42,46); he is therefore presumably a resident of Jerusalem who has known Jesus for some time.[234] The use by the crowd of branches, if these were palm branches (Jn 12.13), at

[232] Ibid. p. 100.
[233] Cf. the quotation from Kennedy on p. 102.
[234] For more extended treatment of this issue cf. Baarlink, as n. 26, p.81.

Jesus' entry to Jerusalem may indicate the autumn feast of Tabernacles, or the feast of Hannukah in December. The cursing of the fig-tree probably belonged to the tradition prior to Mark and if it took place near Jerusalem this indicates a visit to Jerusalem when the figs were ripe, i.e., the autumn. By his arrangement of material Mark appears to wish to make a strong contrast between Jerusalem and the other areas, summarized in the name Galilee, where Jesus also worked. Some of the material Mark sets in Jerusalem could have happened elsewhere, e.g. the content of the disputes with the Jewish leaders in chap 12, the warnings and prophecies of the Little Apocalypse. Were no miracles performed in Jerusalem? It is also possible to see the material as organized in such a way that the miracles practically disappear after Peter's confession in 8.27ff.; following it there are only three and there is a special reason, not connected to the miraculous, for the appearance of each: the healing of the demon-possessed boy (9.14–29) figures as part of the instruction of the disciples (see especially 9.28f.); the healing of blind Bartimaeus (10.46–52) at the end of the journey to Jerusalem and the cursing of the fig-tree (11.12–14,20) are both used with symbolic meaning. The remainder of the miracles are grouped almost entirely between 4.35 and 8.22; those which precede this section usually also have symbolic meaning.

Probably it is impossible to define what it is which holds the material together. If we say of a drama that it is made into a unity by its plot it is doubtful if we are really saying anything profound; but take away the plot and the drama falls apart. In the same way it is the 'plot' which holds Mark together. Plots can be summarised but in the process they lose much of their significance. The plot never exists apart from the content. Later we shall try to outline the Gospel; such an outline may be regarded as the plot, in effect the glue or cement which unifies the Gospel.

CHAPTER XVII

THE NATURE OF MARK'S AUTHORSHIP

(5) Those who write on biblical books are usually faced with the question of the identity of the author; much more important in the case of the second Gospel is the nature of the authorship, and to this we now turn. How did the writer exercise his authorship? The nature of authorship is different in a novel, a poem, a biography, even in a translation (consider what the critics say of Fitzgerald's translation of Omar Khayyam; how much of the original survived in the translation?)

Anyone who writes, writes under some constraints. To communicate a language must be used which at least some other people understand and there must be a cultural frame of reference which is common to author and readers. There are also internal constraints. A novelist might seem to be most free of all but how often in reviews of novels do we not read 'The present work follows the general pattern of X's novels'. A few novelists, e.g., Graham Greene, may succeed in writing two different types of novel but this is unusual. Equally in relation to biographers we often read in reviews 'This follows the general pattern of approach which the author established in earlier biographies'. Novelists and biographers are also caught in the trap that having produced one or two successful works their publishers and readers expect them to continue in the same pattern so that their books will sell. Some of the other constraints come because the authors belong to particular cultures, have had particular upbringing and hold particular beliefs. Others come because they make a conscious decision to approach their subject from a particular angle: they may write as reporters seeking simply to give the facts and let them speak for themselves (whether this is ever possible or not is another matter); they may instead attempt to produce the overall picture they want (e.g., Lytton Strachey's *Eminent Victorians* and *Queen Victoria*). There is the contrast of photograph and caricature; which gives the deeper insight into character? All the time we read we may be conscious of the author's presence (how often in a review of a biography do we read 'You learn a great deal more about the author than about the chosen subject') or we may be hardly conscious of the author at all. The author may indeed deliberately introduce himself or herself into the book; in the story of the young man who ran away (Mk 14.51f.) some have argued that Mark was deliberately intruding himself into his story.[235]

Before we enter on our discussion of the nature of Mark's authorship we need to look at a not unrelated problem in respect of the authorship of 1 Peter. Observing the quality of the Greek in the letter and assuming that a simple fisherman from Galilee could never have written so well, many conclude that he employed Silvanus to write for him; the thoughts are those of Peter but the words are those of Silvanus. We do not need to enter into the arguments for and against such a view but instead let us suppose it is true and ask in what way Peter and Silvanus are the authors of the book? I have a friend who works for a corporation which is bilingual (French and English); its head speaks only French; sometimes he needs to communicate with all the members of the corporation and sometimes only with those who speak English. In the first case he himself composes in French what he wants to say and my friend translates it into English for the English speaking section of the corporation. In the second case he instructs my friend in the general line he is to take and leaves him to write what is necessary. My friend says that his friends can invariably detect when he has composed the communication and when he has simply translated what was given to him. Words, concepts and thoughts are all so inter-related that it is impossible to separate them from one another. What would have been the role of Silvanus in respect of 1 Peter? Was Silvanus the author? An exactly similar problem arises when a reporter 'ghosts' the book of a sports personality; who is the author?

Let us return to Mark. There is an immediate and direct application. According to traditional ideas Mark was the interpreter of Peter.[236] Simplistic views see Mark as sitting at Peter's feet and writing down what he said; more complex theories see Mark as writing up after the death of Peter the stories that he knew Peter had regularly told of Jesus. Few today would hold to the simple transcriptional point of view; if we accept the other in how far is Mark the author of the Gospel? Since those who adhere to the view of Mark as in some way the interpreter of Peter normally also hold the view that the Gospel is historically reliable we are faced with the question how far is a historian an author? A novelist can be said to create his own material; this of course has to be qualified since his material arises out of his experience of the world; a historian has to work with material that is provided for him, from which he

---

[235] But see above pp. 26f.
[236] See above pp. 21–8 for fuller discussion of this issue.

can select, but which he ought not to create. Or is it legitimate for him to amalgamate two or three incidents to create an incident which never happened but which shows in short space an essential trait of his subject? Clearly the quality of the biographer's and novelist's authorship will differ. Did Mark include all the stories Peter told? Did he include only those which he knew from experience the church in Rome liked to rehear continually? Did he play up or play down the weaknesses of Peter? If he was not a simple translator there were many areas into which his authorship would enter.

Seemingly at the opposite extreme to such views are those of the form critics, though in fact the role of Mark as author receives as little emphasis with them as it does with those who view him as the interpreter of Peter. A. Menzies and K.L. Schmidt likened the separate stories of the Gospel to pearls on a string or cord.[237] The string was relatively unimportant; the pearls were all-important. We require to give more attention to the string than they did.

How did the Gospel come into existence? The community can be given the most important role. It preserved the different stories of Jesus; it shaped their form; it adapted them to its own interests. It began to gather them together. Isolated sayings of Jesus were strung into sequences; parables were associated with one another; chains of miracle stories appeared. The Gospels are the final product of this work of the community. The Gospel of Mark arose through sociological pressure rather than as the result of the desire of an author to compose. Thus R. Bultmann writes:

> There is no definable boundary between the oral and written tradition, and similarly the process of the editing of the material of the tradition was beginning already before it had been fixed in a written form. . . . But since it (the composition of the Gospels) involves nothing in principle new, but only completes what was begun in the oral tradition, it can only be considered in organic connection with the history of the material as it lay before the Evangelists.[238]

Similarly M. Dibelius:

> The literary understanding of the synoptics begins with the recognition that they are collections of material. The composers are only to the smallest extent authors. . . . In reality the personal factors had

---

[237] Although the image is usually attributed to Schmidt, 'Die Stellung der Evangelien in der allgemeinen Literaturgeschichte', in *EUCHARISTERION* (Festschrift für H. Gunkel, FRLANT 19.2) Göttingen, 1923, it is in fact found earlier in A. Menzies, *The Earliest Gospel*, London, 1901, p. 29.

[238] Op. cit. (see n. 88), p. 321.

> but little significance in shaping the tradition, at any rate as far as the Gospels of Mark and Matthew are concerned, and it is very doubtful whether much depended upon the personal factor in the earlier history of the tradition.[239]

The Palestinian community had preserved the Jesus material; the Hellenistic community had a kerygma; the two had to come together at some stage; their inevitable marriage produced the gospel form of Mark. The marriage however was not so much the work of an individual as that of the community itself.[240]

Today redaction criticism has produced a new picture and Mark is once again regarded as an author. His Gospel is not the result of inevitable sociological forces but his creation. But before we react too strongly against the form critics we should recognize that much that we want to say was implicit in what they wrote though they did not stress it. When pearls are put on a string there is a new totality which the same pearls lying in a box do not possess. Thus the Gospel was something new over and above the separate incidents which existed in the tradition. And when the pearls are put on a string they also are set in a relation to one another and, we might say, their beauty enhanced; when the incidents of the Gospel are put together they bring out in each other points that were not previously observed. The simplest example of this are the sandwiches created by Mark.

When we turn to the actual work of the redaction critics some startling differences appear as to the extent of Mark's activity as author. As an extreme example on one side we may take W.H. Kelber's discussion of the Gethsemane incident. He concludes by saying

> With the possible exception of the Gethsemane lament and prayer tradition (i.e. vv. 36,38, but not even all of these) the pericope is fully explicable in terms of Markan linguistic and syntactical features, literary devices, as well as religious motifs.[241]

He also says that in the case of 'the place whose name was Gethsemane' we have 'the bedrock of a pre-Markan tradition'. Taken incident by incident in this way the greater part of the material can be attributed to Mark as his creation.

But a conservative approach is also possible. W.L. Lane[242]

---

[239] *From Tradition to Gospel* (ET by B.E. Woolf) London, 1934, pp. 3,4.

[240] For detailed criticism of this view see Güttgemanns, as n. 10, passim.

[241] 'Mark 14.32–42: Gethsemane – Passion Christology and Discipleship Failure', *ZNW* 63 (1972) 166–187 at p. 176.

[242] *The Gospel according to Mark,* London, 1974.

accepts a redaction-critical position but he rarely sees Mark's hand within particular pericopae; none of the incidents and little within them are therefore to be attributed to Mark.

Neither of these positions need be accepted. When Mark retells a story which he has taken from the tradition it is natural that he should allow some of his own words and stylistic characteristics to appear in it; it is practically impossible to retell stories without this happening. We should not therefore be surprised to find Markan characteristics within pericopae. But also in whatever community Mark worked the stories from the tradition were already known; it would therefore be hazardous for him to make great alterations in them, even more hazardous to invent new pericopae. In communities where story tellers function orally sociological pressures maintain the main outline and most of the details of stories; change only takes place gradually. This sociological pressure would continue even into the time when the story was first written down.

If this is so then we must look for Mark's authorship in the framework and selection of the material rather than in the stories as such. So far as the framework goes the form critics argued that it was that of the Hellenistic kerygma; this is so slender a framework that it may be safely ignored. C.H. Dodd argued for a much more detailed framework, but this is difficult to accept.[243] More recently as we have seen it has been argued that Mark's framework was provided by the canons of rhetorical or dramatic criticism. This of course allows for the creation of the framework by Mark. It is however unlikely that Mark had the necessary training in rhetoric or drama, which were taught only in the tertiary stage of education in the ancient world.[244] Mark's Greek suggests that he never got beyond the primary stage. But anyone who has a knowledge of primitive story tellers or of uneducated people narrating events knows that it seems to come quite naturally to some of them to give a relatively strong framework to the whole and to produce something which sounds quite dramatic. Indeed educated people often fail to produce this dramatic result even though the story they tell contains it within itself. The point being made here is that what Mark has created as author is a 'whole'. In every whole the parts relate to one another and yet the whole itself has a point to it which is not the same as the point of any of its separate parts. It is true that many of the stories which Mark tells are recounted vividly but the whole has also its own vividness and Mark's contribution lies not only in the vivid telling of particular incidents but also in the vivid

[243] See above, pp. 6, 100.
[244] See above, p. 104 and n. 219.

nature of the whole. Mark has therefore done much more than fix the oral tradition in writing;[245] he has created a new unity. We shall look at the nature of this unity later.

It is probably easier to achieve wholeness if the writer starts from scratch as the novelist does and creates the incidents which he wants to make the parts of his whole. Mark however did not begin in this way but used the material which came to him in the tradition. (In the tradition the natural way in which it originally cohered in the life of the 'hero' had already been lost.[246]) This makes his creation of a whole more susprising. It is here that his real contribution lies as author.

To move to another point: authors can have different relations to what they create. They may be and can remain entirely external to their material. In so far as they have not themselves taken part in any of the incidents which they record they must always be more or less external. The compiler of the letters of some great man of the past who only puts them in chronological order and writes some explanatory footnotes remains external to the material in a way that the biographer of the same man does not. Fiction writers can never be said to be external to what they write since they do not record things that happened anywhere other than in their own minds; they are the only people who have entered into the experiences of their characters and know their thoughts and feelings; anyone else who does so can only do that through what the novelist writes. Clearly also in autobiographies writers are largely internal to the material about themselves but are external to other material. Biographers are in a different position. On the one hand they are external to their material since it concerns someone else and the incidents of his or her life; on the other hand few biographers are mere reporters. They attempt to analyse and then synthesise their material; they deduce the inner thoughts of characters from their actions and supply reasons why on certain occasions they acted in particular ways. There is an essential difference here from writers of fiction who are in a sense absolutely free; provided they keep their characters internally consistent and allow for development in character, they can decide beforehand what kind of personality they wish to attribute to each. Biographers are always tied down by the material which comes to them.

It is clear that Mark as author comes much nearer to the biographer than the novelist. He attributes[247] motives and inner

---

[245] Cf. Güttgemanns, as n. 10, p. 124.

[246] See above, pp. 3–6.

[247] Cf. N.R. Petersen, ' "Point of View" in Mark's Narrative', *Semeia*, 12 (1978) 97–121.

thoughts to his characters in incidents at which he cannot have been present: in 2.6,7 he says that the scribes question the activity of Jesus in forgiving the paralytic, in 5.29 that a woman 'felt in her body that she was healed of her disease'; in 6.19 he implies that Herodias acted out of a grudge. He attributes thoughts to Jesus: at 1.41 either pity or anger[248] in relation to the leper, at 6.34 compassion on the crowd. At 14.36 he even attributes a prayer to Jesus in Gethsemane which no one had heard. Mark thus enters into the thoughts and feelings of his characters; in that way he makes himself internal to the story. But he is also clearly external to it for he sets it in a past time and, if he is writing in Rome, in another area of the world. He also fails, as we shall see below, on many occasions to attribute thoughts to Jesus.

When Mark is internal to the story and intrudes his own judgements upon what people thought and felt he does so in order to interpret the events he reports. All authors make some kind of moral and theological judgements. The kind of people about whom they write is itself a judgement of some kind. Biographers assess their central character and in passing will evaluate other characters who come into their story. There are few 'good' characters in Mark; perhaps the centurion who at the the cross says 'Truly this man was son of God' is the only one on whose character no stain is cast. All the others appear either to misunderstand Jesus, to reject his claims on them, or to be hostile to him, and Mark is critical of them all. This serves to point out the goodness of the central character. It can therefore be assumed that Mark considers his own moral and theological judgements would agree with those of Jesus. In what Jesus does and in what he teaches Mark sees meaning for those for whom he writes. But it would be wrong to think that Mark is merely critical of all the others in his story. Some of those who fail or misunderstand are in the end restored; this is the significance of the message to the women at the tomb to go and tell Peter and his disciples where they are to meet him.

We have implied here that the central character is Jesus. It might be argued that the central character in the story of Mark is God. Jesus acts according to the will of God as the story of Gethsemane shows; Peter is rebuked for being on the side of men and not of God (8.33); both at the beginning and at the end of the story Jesus is described as 'the son of God'. But perhaps the distinction is a quibble, and that itself may say something about Mark's view of Jesus.

Most authors when they write think of the effect of what they

---

[248] Dependent on the reading of the text in 1.41.

write on their readers. A few poets may write for their own self-indulgence and to explicate to themselves their own feelings but this is not generally true. Authors who think of their readers think in different ways. Novelists, or at least popular novelists, think of how their readers will enjoy what they write and may include pornographic material to titillate them. Some biographers by telling the story of a favourite character may even hope to raise the moral level of the lives of their readers. When Mark wrote he had his readers in mind and he told his stories so that he might deepen their Christian experience.

Two further points should be made here. First, if a writing is to be acceptable to those who read it it must present a believable world. Most literature deals with people who can be imagined as living in the world we know. Some literature however moves out of our normal world; science fiction projects us into a world of the future yet it always has sufficient common features with our world for us to believe it is a real world; even 'Alice in Wonderland' presents us with a world which, as we read the book, still seems to be something that is possible. From another angle this means that writer and readers must be able to share the world which is being written about: they must have a common area of shared knowledge and experience. Not everything can be shared and the author may have to go out of his way to explain certain features of the world he presents; thus Mark interprets Aramaic words and Jewish customs for his readers. A shared world however means the writer can refer indirectly to events of which he does not directly speak knowing his readers will understand; thus Mark in reporting the prophecy of John the Baptizer that Jesus will baptize with the Holy Spirit can assume that his readers know of the activity of the Spirit in the church since Pentecost. When the young man at the tomb instructs the women to go and tell Peter and the disciples that Jesus goes ahead of them into Galilee (16.7) readers know that Peter and the disciples met up again with the risen Jesus. In his report of the Last Supper Mark does not need to stress its regular repetition because his readers already practise this repetition.

Secondly, all authors and readers share some common experience since they are human; in the case of a Christian author writing for Christians they will also share the Christian experience. If then Mark is writing, not for outsiders, but for Christians he will know that he and they together share a certain experience of Christ. He knows that they will give a special position to Christ and though he may redefine and explain this position he can assume its existence; he knows that together he and they experience a certain separation from the world. Unless we have strong evidence to the contrary we can always assume that a writer and his readers (or hearers) have the beliefs common to the type of group to which they belong. Rightwing conservative groups and leftwing socialist groups may together share some common beliefs but the rightwing groups on their part will share a much wider circle of beliefs among themselves, as on their part will the leftwing groups. We may therefore assume that any group of Christians in the first century will share some common beliefs and that the person who writes to them will also share these beliefs. Where he appears deliberately to be stressing a particular belief it may be because he differs from all of them or from some particular sub-group within them or from some group outside them which he envisages as leading them astray. We would need very strong evidence in a particular writing before we supposed that the author or the group to which he was writing believed Jesus died by strangulation and not crucifixion or that the group did not accept some resurrection belief about Jesus, e.g. that he had appeared to the disciples; if the author believed in something markedly different on a major issue from the group he would need to argue it very vehemently if they were to be convinced of it, and if we were to be persuaded that he really was arguing for it. As a working hypothesis we therefore assume that Mark and his readers shared the main beliefs of Christians of the first century.

Earlier we saw attempts to understand Mark through the use of the rhetorical and dramatic conventions of his day. Attempts have also been made to understand the Gospel by means of modern literary theories. N.R. Petersen has been prominent in applying these and we shall look at two important contributions he has made to the nature of Mark's authorship.

In his first[249] contribution Petersen says that 'Mark's narrative belongs to that type of third-person point of view known as the omniscient point of view of an intrusive narrator'. In dependence on M.H. Abrams[250] he seems to mean that the Gospel approximates to a work of fiction in which the narrator knows everything that needs to be known about the characters and events, that he can dispose of them in the narrative as he wishes and that he has a 'privileged' access to their feelings and motives. Intrusive narrators are those who not only report, but also freely comment on their characters and their activities. Petersen says that 'Mark's rhetoric is the rhetoric of fiction'[251] and concludes that we must regard Mark as a narrator rather than a redactor.[252]

---

[249] Art. cit. (n. 247), p. 105.
[250] *A Glossary of Literary Terms*, New York, 1971.
[251] Art. cit. (n. 247), p. 115.
[252] Art. cit. (n. 247), p. 118.

It is interesting that he nowhere defines what he means by either 'narrative' or 'narrator'. The kind of evidence which he adduces to support his theory, e.g., that Mark knows the inner thoughts of the people in his accounts, is equally true of the historians of the ancient world who regularly wrote the speeches of those whose history they were retailing. This then cannot be a significant point in distinguishing between history and fiction, or indeed between biography and fiction. Mark moreover is not as omniscient in respect of the narrative as Petersen supposes for it is quite easy to detect differences between his point of view and that of the underlying material.[253]

As we have just seen Mark certainly does sometimes attribute motives and words to his characters but he often fails to do this and it is useful to look at the places where he has not done so. Nothing is said at the baptism about what went on in the minds of Jesus and John; it was not long before others began to fill in the gaps (Mt 3.14f.); the same is true of the temptation (Mt 4.1–11; Lk 4.1–13). Writers of lives of Jesus and preachers have not failed to supply what Mark left unsaid. Mark wrote 6.52 and set in it one of his main themes (the hardness of heart of the disciples); we might have expected him to go on and add something about Jesus' disappointment with his disciples. Throughout the passion Jesus is almost entirely silent speaking only three times (14.62; 15.2,34); the last of these is not for Mark an expression of his inner feelings but a theological statement. Again during his trial we never learn what he thought of his judges or those who crucified him. His words at Gethsemane which appear important come from the tradition and not from Mark. This is also true of most of what we earlier drew attention to. When motives and words already lay in the tradition Mark took them over; where they did not he did not create them. If he was an omniscient author he appears to have kept his omniscience to himself. We must also allow for the fact, and this is most important, that Mark is using material which was known to his community; Petersen treats Mark as if he lived and worked in a vacuum. Since Mark's material came to him from within his community he was not free to change it at will. We must therefore reject any suggestion of omniscience on his part. He is neither an author in the ordinarily understood sense of that word, nor a simple redactor; his work lies somewhere between the two.

In his second contribution[254] Petersen looks for the 'plot' in the Gospel. We would largely agree with him 'that Mark unquestion-

---

[253] See above pp. 12f.
[254] *Literary Criticism for New Testament Critics*, Philadelphia, 1978.

ably and self-consciously plots his narrative . . .'[255] though we would disagree with the way he understands this for we doubt if the literary theory which he applies to the Gospel really reveals the true nature of its plot and if Mark acted as self-consciously as he supposes.[256] Standaert as we have seen[257] attempts to explain the Gospel through a theory of composition which was prevalent in the first century; Petersen attempts to do so through a current theory of literary criticism. In accordance with this theory about narrative he looks for temporal marks within the Gospel pointing forward or backward. But there are also geographical marks and he ignores these; they however are important; Mark uses as a marker 'on the way' and other geographical references; together they help to provide a structure to the book.[258] Strangely also Petersen pays no attention to many of the deliberate temporal marks which Mark appears to have introduced into the material or which lay in the material before he used it, e.g. the six days referring to the date of the transfiguration (9.1), the day-by-day dating of events in the last week of Jesus' life. More seriously by paying attention only to temporal marking it seems that Petersen is bound to end up with a plan for the book which pays attention to 'time' and that means either a *heilsgeschichtliche* or an apocalyptic view; clearly the first would be difficult to work out in the case of Mark and so Petersen opts for the second. If we take into account both the temporal markers and the geographical markers then we see that the thrust forward in Mark is much more towards the cross and the resurrection than towards the parousia; Petersen however practically ignores the cross and the resurrection in his attempt to find evidence for the parousia. We have already seen that there are good reasons to suppose that Mark wished to deflate apocalyptic hopes rather than to intensify them.[259]

Petersen's literary approach also involves the assumption that Mark is to be decoded apart from its historical situation. With a novel there is perhaps no other way in which to work, though even this is not always true; Tolstoy's *War and Peace* needs to be read in the light of contemporary events. If however we are examining a 'history' or 'biography' where we are concerned with events belonging to a world outside the written text we cannot ignore their external context. This is particularly true when events are involved

---

[255] Op. cit., p. 58.
[256] See below, pp. 128ff. for discussion.
[257] See above, pp. 101ff.
[258] See pp. 84ff., 129f.
[259] See above pp. 41–3.

of which both readers (hearers) and writer know and when there are common experiences in which they share. The real context for interpretation must include them, their knowledge and their experience as well as the written text. For the readers 1.8 does not point forward to 13.11 as Petersen suggests[260] but to Pentecost, an event lying outside the Gospel; indeed the readers may never even have noticed the connection of 1.8 and 13.11 within the Gospel. There is much in the Gospel which is fulfilled outside it. The downfall of the betrayer is prophesied (14.21) but no account is given. Whatever interpretation is given to 14.28 and 16.7 no fulfilment is found within the Gospel. The women are instructed to tell Peter and the disciples that Jesus is risen (16.7f.); they must have done so or the incident would not be known. The Last Supper reaches out into the eucharistic worship of the community. The disciples are instructed to heal by prayer (9.28f.) but we have no instances of them doing so. They are sent to be 'fishers of men'; it is only in the life of the church that this is carried out. Thus within the Gospel we are continually pointed outside and beyond it.

Essentially what Petersen has ignored is the shared experience and information of writer and readers and what we may term the 'exhortatory' nature of the writing. But Petersen also argues as if Mark had an absolutely free hand with the material. Not all the temporal markers come from Mark's hand; some were already present within the material as it came to him. John the Baptizer must be introduced prior to Jesus for this was the way he was regarded in Christian tradition and in actual fact his mission began before that of Jesus; the Last Supper belonged to the passion long before Mark wrote; the transfiguration took place six days after some event (9.2). The plot was therefore in part pre-determined; Mark was not its complete master.

What is most disappointing about Petersen's approach is his failure to provide fresh insights into our understanding of the Gospel. It may be that he has chosen the wrong literary model. A clue to this may lie in the general recognition, which Petersen shares,[261] that Mark has a purpose. The kind of purpose which drives Mark on whether it be to polemicize against heresy or to act as a pastor to his people is not the kind of purpose which is normally found in literature. Where there is such a purpose we are inevitably driven outside the book and therefore we need more than the book itself in order to understand it.

---

[260] Op. cit., p. 71.
[261] Op. cit. (as n. 254), pp. 78ff.

It is perhaps appropriate at this point to consider the nature of the 'wholeness' which pertains to the Gospel. Many scholars argue quite correctly that Mark should be regarded as a whole and point out that too much time and energy have been devoted to dissecting it into tradition and redaction. Any move to regard the Gospel as a 'whole' must be encouraged. Later we shall attempt to draw out the nature of the 'wholeness'.[262] In the meantime however it is necessary to clarify what we mean by the term and to see what limitations must be placed on it. We saw earlier[263] that when Mark used tradition he tended to preserve it in the form he received it even though it might at points conflict with his own views. Any wholeness therefore must allow for a certain element of inconsistency. Certain elements which belong to the wholeness are not expressed within the wholeness because they belong to the shared experience and knowledge of writer and readers. If I pick up a letter in the street I may be able to understand part of it but to understand it all I need to know something of the world of the writer and the reader; the writer can leave many things unsaid because the reader knows them. Another way of putting this is to say that the Gospel has features which reach out beyond itself, hooks as it were by which it latches itself on to the general Christian experience of the time. The wholeness for which we look is not simply an artistic wholeness but one which arises out of its 'purpose'. In a novel or poem we may look for an artistic wholeness but the wholeness for which we look in a theological treatise or an essay in ethics is of a different nature. This is particularly true if the latter are not merely exercises in thinking but intended to change the beliefs and behaviour of their readers. Mark is a narrative and we may look for something of the nature of the wholeness of a narrative in Mark but Mark is more than narrative and therefore we must also look for a wholeness which includes its theology and ethics. Its wholeness must be judged from all these points of view. Mark tells his story in order to change his community.

We must now try to sum up; if Mark is neither author nor editor what then is he? Previously in discussing his authorship I have suggested that he was like an artist putting together a collage,[264] creating a new unity out of existing material. A better illustration[265] may be that of a composer who brings together folk songs or sea

---

[262] See below, pp. 128ff.

[263] See pp. 12f.

[264] 'Mark's Preservation of the Tradition' (as n. 24).

[265] This suggestion was made to me during the course of a seminar at the British Conference of New Testament scholars held in Glasgow University, September, 1980. I forgot to note who made the suggestion: I hope he or she will forgive me.

shanties[266] to make a new unity. Just as each of the original tunes is clearly recognisable but each has also been subtily changed to accommodate to it what precedes and follows so Mark created a new and exciting whole out of the material available to him in the tradition. He has conserved material, but it would be wrong to say that this was what he primarily set out to do. He has used the tradition, but used it creatively. We go on then to look at the nature of his creative use and the resulting unity.

[266] E.g. Henry Wood's 'Fantasia for Orchestra on British Sea-Songs'.

CHAPTER XVIII

WHY A GOSPEL?

(6) We may open up the way into the question of the nature of the writing by asking why Mark wrote what he wrote and not something else. If he was writing as a pastor would not a homily have been more appropriate? The author of 'To the Hebrews' thought so. If Mark wished to help his people would a sermon in the modern sense of that word not have been more suitable? Both homily and sermon could have included incidents from the life of Jesus as illustrations to drive points home. The incidents were already being used in that way for pastoral purposes within the community. Alternatively, why did Mark not compile a handbook of the teaching of Jesus so that through direct instruction his readers might appreciate and act out the words of Jesus? Perhaps this last question can be answered more easily. Mark does indeed emphasise Jesus as teacher but he gives less of his actual teaching than we would wish; what Jesus does is more important than what he teaches. A handbook of his teaching would not have brought out for Mark's readers the way in which Jesus helps and cares for them.

It is comparatively easy at this point to say that Mark wrote something which was so wholly and completely new that it is impossible to categorize it in terms of any existing genre; the genre 'gospel' was created by Mark. For the moment we bypass the implicit question of the newness of the genre; our answer will appear as we go on. One way of taking seriously the narrative form of Mark and of bringing it into line with an existing category is to describe it as a biography. Two attempts have recently been made in this respect.

We commence with G.N. Stanton[267] who argues that gospel material was always a part of missionary preaching. He instances both Paul's awareness of material about Jesus and his appeals to the character of Jesus and the references to the life of Jesus in some of the missionary sermons of Acts.[268] Mark was therefore only taking a little further a process which was already in being. There

---

[267] *Jesus of Nazareth in New Testament Preaching* (SNTS Monograph Series 27), Cambridge, 1974.

[268] Op. cit., pp. 86ff.

must be doubts about this. Paul uses the Jesus-tradition but only very occasionally does he refer to it as such; while he employs some of the sayings of Jesus he rarely puts Jesus' name behind them. Stanton both fails to explain why this material is not specified as Jesus-tradition and he over-exaggerates its extent. Further when Paul does appeal to the character of Jesus it is in passages like the Philippian hymn (Phil 2.6–11) and 2 Cor 8.9 where it is the love and humility of the pre-incarnate Jesus rather than of the incarnate which are stressed. Finally it is by no means as certain as Stanton assumes[269] that the sermons of Acts reflect the preaching of the community prior to Mark; they may reflect much more that of Luke's own day. Apart from all this while Stanton may suggest that the Gospel was a natural form to evolve through Christian interest in the historical Jesus he accepts enough of the form-critical approach to make it difficult to explain the arrangement of much of the material in Mark once it had lost its anchorage in chronological history. Here he justifies the Evangelists through parallels from contemporary literature:[270] those who wrote 'lives' in ancient times adopted different principles from the writers of modern biographies; they did not write chronologically; incidents were placed alongside one another because they illustrated the same point though they might come from different periods in the subject's life. Modern biographies are often dominated by the financial needs of their authors (written to entertain) or their curiosity (academic research) but rarely written to set out their subjects as models; ancient lives were used to recommend good and bad ways of living. The Evangelists are certainly thus much closer to ancient biographers than to modern; an attempt to instruct by telling the story of someone's life would have been easily acceptable to the ancient world. In the end Stanton seems to answer the question why the Gospels were written by implying that this was done in order that men should know who this Jesus was who was crucified and risen.[271] It is impossible to deny that this may not have been a part of what the evangelists intended but there is a great deal more in Mark, especially in those parts where we may trace his own hand and which are devoted to disentangling the significance of Jesus rather than to providing information about his life and character. That the Gospels incidentally answer the question who Jesus was does not of itself mean that they were written for that purpose. Standaert[272] makes three additional criticisms of Stanton: (i) Stan-

[269] Op. cit., pp. 67ff.
[270] Op. cit., pp. 117ff.
[271] Op. cit., pp. 180ff.
[272] Op. cit. (as n. 11), pp. 433ff.

ton treats all the Gospels in the same way but they are different; the argument for Matthew and Luke as biographies is stronger than for Mark; the Gospels need to be considered separately. To be fair to Stanton it must be said that he bases his study on Luke and only briefly extends it to the other Gospels. (ii) Biographies were written by educated authors for educated readers; Mark's Gospel neither appears to be by an educated person nor written for educated readers. (iii) Mark's Gospel lacks many of the standard features of biographies, e.g., details of birth, physical description. We cannot then agree with Stanton that Mark's writing is best categorised as 'biography'.

C.H. Talbert[273] like Stanton classes the Gospels with the biographies of the ancient world pointing out the difference between ancient and modern biography. He examines and rejects the arguments of Bultmann and others for the Gospels as a unique genre. These arguments stress the highly mythical, cultic and world-negating nature of our canonical Gospels and lead to the conclusion that these features make them unlike anything else that was known in the ancient world.

Talbert has very little difficulty in disposing of the last of these characteristics.[274] There is no reason why an eschatological perspective with a negative attitude to the world should itself imply the rejection of secular literary genres; Paul who had such an attitude used the secular literary form of the 'letter'. In respect of the other two points Talbert argues that ancient biography could, and often did, possess mythical features and have a cultic situation. Ancient biographies show men as miraculously born or taken up into heaven after a good life to become immortals; here there are clear similarities to the Synoptic Gospels. A different form of myth, one which was also found in ancient biography, controls the Fourth Gospel, the myth of a descending and ascending Redeemer, though not necessarily in a gnostic form.[275] The Synoptic Gospels depend in varying degrees on the myths of the divine man and of the immortals. In relation to the cultic situation of biographies Talbert points to the place of biography in recounting the lives of philosophers within philosophical schools and the lives of the founders of cities and nations; in neither case is their use purely secular but has a religious flavour. In the case of philosophers their lives and their teaching are often brought together. He indicates that biographies were written for different purposes in the ancient world and classes Mark amongst those whose aim was 'to dispel a

[273] *What is a Gospel? The Genre of the Canonical Gospels,* London, 1978.
[274] Op. cit., pp. 115ff.
[275] Op. cit., pp. 39, 42, 53ff.

false image of the teacher and to provide a true model to follow'.[276]

He writes again: Mark 'was written to defend against a misunderstanding of the church's saviour and to portray a true image of him for the disciples to follow. This Gospel was written in terms of the myth of immortals. This gives the story of Jesus its overall structure and indicates that the Gospel functioned as a myth of origins for an early Christian community'.[277]

The early Christians clearly used existing literary genres and there is no virtue in arguing that the Gospels, because they are about the son of God, must necessarily use a genre other than one which already existed.[278] Biographies both literary and popular were well-known in the ancient world and anyone who set out to write about Jesus would be bound to be influenced in some way by them, though that would not necessarily mean that he set out consciously to imitate them. Talbert and Stanton have done sufficient to show that there are similarities between ancient biographies and the canonical gospels, but that of itself does not mean that we should classify the latter as biographies. While ancient biographies had mythical and cultic features it may be queried whether they manifest them to as high a degree as do the canonical gospels. At what point does a difference in degree result in a difference of genre? Probably, as with Stanton, Talbert's case is strongest in respect of the Gospel of Luke.[279] In relation to the cultic characteristics of ancient biography and of the canonical gospels Talbert does not enquire whether and in how far each was used to nurture the faithful or for outside apologetic purposes. Nor does he enquire what features of ancient biography are missing from the canonical gospels. He writes 'Biography was interested in the individual's character, his involvement in a historical process being important only in so far as it reveals his essence'.[280] The canonical gospels cannot be said to be interested in the character of Jesus.[281]

Turning more directly to Mark it can be seen that what Talbert describes as the function of Mark is at variance with the view we have been proposing. The divine origin of the 'hero' and the

---

[276] Op. cit., p. 94.

[277] Op. cit., p. 134.

[278] On the genre of the Gospels see below pp. 140ff.

[279] Cf. H.C. Kee, *Christian Origins in Sociological Perspective* (London, 1980), pp. 146f.

[280] Talbert, op. cit., p. 16.

[281] In discussing Talbert's work I have been able to draw on the vast knowledge of my colleague P.G. Walsh, Professor of Humanity in the University of Glasgow, though he is of course not responsible for anything I have written. For a thorough and exhaustive examination of Talbert's views see now D.E. Aune, 'The Problem of the Genre of the Gospels: A Critique of C.H. Talbert's What is a Gospel?' in *Gospel Perspectives,* Vol II (ed. R.T. France and David Wenham), Sheffield, 1981, pp. 9–60.

'ascent' theme which Talbert regards as important parts of the myth of the immortals are missing from Mark. Jesus does not ascend at the end of the Gospel and leave the church to itself but is continuously present with it through his words and actions. Nor did Mark write to defend Jesus against a misunderstanding of his nature; his purpose was pastoral rather than polemical. The element of imitation in the Gospel is small; it is from disciples rather than Jesus that we learn about conduct. The Gospel does not function as a myth of origins for an early Christian community. Curiously in Talbert's discussion and comparison of ancient biography and the Gospels almost nothing is said of the central position which the cross occupies in the Gospels; its central position in Mark has indeed often been used to argue that Mark's Gospel is in fact a deliberate correction of any 'divine man' theme.

It could also be said that Talbert undervalues the 'biblical' nature of the Gospels. Not only do they provide theology through narrative but they exhibit many of the literary qualities of pre-Christian non-canonical Jewish writings; these themselves stand in the tradition of biblical writing. In the discussion following Silberman's paper at the San Antonio Colloquy on the Gospels James A. Sanders suggests that these similarities include a common interest in

> (1) a message for the times and a messenger; (2) a congruity between the message and the messenger (and at times an incongruity as well); (3) the effect that the message has on the messenger's life and fate; (4) the effect that the message and messenger have on the people and on the various symbols and institutions of society; and (5) the words and works of the messenger. These features can be found in the book of Jeremiah; they can be found in the books of Moses; they are also found in the gospels (with the addition of the Crucifixion and the Resurrection). This suggests that the gospels wish to be understood as 'biblical books', that is, as standing in the line of the earlier tradition about what God has done. Their basic theocentrism (see Sanders' response to Silberman, p.236) reveals that they *are* biblical books and expressions of a Jewish pluralism. In addition, there is their widespread use of the Old Testament: quotations (with and without introductory formulas), phrases, allusions, and themes; indeed, there is even the same shape of individual units.[282]

As with Stanton we have to conclude that Mark cannot be categorised as 'biography'. But we must thank both Stanton and Talbert for insisting again on the 'historical' aspect of the book.

[282] In Walker, as n. 6, p. 244.

CHAPTER XIX

THE DRAMA OF THE GOSPEL

(7) If the Gospel is 'historical', i.e. has a sequence of events, it is proper to bring this out by means of a summary. First we need to recall Mark's share in creating the sequence of events. Part of that sequence was inherent in the tradition as it came to him but in part it has been created by him. Any sequence in which incidents are placed other than haphazardly sets them in relation to one another so that they throw light on each other. Since for Mark the most important part of the story is the death and resurrection of Jesus he has been able to relate almost all of the incidents to this event. Every storyteller when he retells a story shapes it to the particular situation in which he finds himself; parts of it which to an earlier audience were immediately explicable have to be paraphrased or explained to a new audience; new sentences will be inserted to bring out points which to the original audience were perfectly obvious (e.g. Mark translates Aramaic phrases); and if the anecdote follows on another anecdote which he has just told or an anecdote which someone else has told or if his anecdote is part of an argument or discussion about a particular theory, then the anecdote has to be adapted to fit into the preceding and following context. It is modified to suit what comes before and what may come after. Thus by drawing the incidents together and adapting them into a larger unity Mark has given to each incident a new flavour, he has produced new meaning from it, a meaning to suit his purpose. In the final issue all the incidents have to be interpreted in the light of the cross and resurrection and the cross and resurrection in their light. The one who is crucified is the one who has been to Gethsemane, has been deserted by his followers though he never forsook them, has cleansed the Temple, has argued with the Pharisees, has angered the people and their rulers, has put forward new views on the Sabbath and on purification. The one who has healed many and fed thousands is the one whom the priests and scribes mocked as he hung on the Cross saying 'He saved others; he cannot save himself'. Thus the sum total of the events as arranged by Mark or as inherent in the tradition makes a greater impact than would the individual incidents reported in haphazard order.

It is important however to recall that certain elements in the tradition could not be freely moved around and placed wherever Mark wished. 1 Cor 11 shows us that the Last Supper was already located in the tradition as taking place during Jesus' last night on earth; Gethsemane could hardly be given a position other than it has. Mark was tied in another way by the tradition; some of it was already gathered into 'complexes' of material of similar nature, e.g. controversy stories (2.1–3.5), parables (4.3–32).

At different points throughout this study we have begun to see that the arrangement of the material in many instances is not however accidental. We saw how Mark created a contrast between Galilee and Jerusalem by bringing Jesus only once to Jerusalem. He makes effective use of his 'sandwich' technique so that the cursing of the fig tree and the cleansing of the Temple (11.12–25) throw light on each other. By ignoring the life of Jesus prior to his baptism by John he makes Jesus appear quite suddenly on the scene and connects his appearance (1.2,3) with the Old Testament so that there is continuity between Jesus and the prophets. The predictions by Jesus of his death and resurrection are so arranged that they form a pilgrimage of Jesus to Jerusalem. By placing the argument among the disciples about which of them is greatest directly after one of these predictions (9.32ff.) he shows how wrong such discussions about greatness are in the light of the cross.

Having indicated the way in which Mark has worked we may now set out in a brief summary the flow of his narrative.

There is a prologue (1.1–15) in which we learn that the story did not begin with Jesus but is a continuation of what is found in the Old Testament; 1.2–3 is indeed the only deliberate quotation from the Old Testament in the Gospel outside the sayings of Jesus. We learn that Jesus will baptise with the Spirit (the readers know that this was fulfilled at Pentecost), that he himself was so baptised, was described as son of God and encountered Satan in a great struggle. His message is then summarised partly in the terms which he himself used (the kingdom of God is at hand) and partly in those of the church (repent and believe the gospel).

This is followed by a long section (1.16–8.26) containing calls to disciples, teaching about the kingdom, mighty deeds or miracles; just what we might expect from the prologue when it is spelt out in detail. But opposition also is aroused and continues to threaten; hints of the ultimate conclusion appear. We are rushed through this section at great speed; it has often been alleged that Mark over-uses the word 'immediately'; it appears 32 times in 1.16–8.26 and only 10 times in the remainder of the Gospel; it has thus an important role in this section of the story.

In the next section (8.27–10.52) the sense of movement is still there but is no longer produced through temporal data but through geographical. We are sent on a journey from Caesarea Philippi through Capernaum and Jericho to Jerusalem. The key phrase is 'on the way' (8.27; 9.33; 10.32,52) and disciples are bidden to follow Jesus on his way. The stages of the journey are marked by reference to areas and towns leading to Jerusalem.

The final section (11.1–16.8) really lacks movement. Jesus is in Jerusalem and what happens to him is made out in terms of days, Sunday, Monday and so on to Friday. On Friday itself we move from early morning to the third hour, to the sixth hour; it is as if there is a countdown through the days of Holy Week and the hours of the last day to the cross itself and then onward to the resurrection on the third day. In the cross the opposition has triumphed, but the church knows of the victory of the resurrection. The disciples fled; again the Church knows that they have been restored. And the story points forward: once more Jesus will be at their head on the way to Galilee as they go on mission.

Seen in this way we realise that Mark is a good story-teller, or, perhaps more correctly, a natural dramatist. When Petersen says Mark 'unquestionably and self-consciously plots his narrative'[283] this suggests too deliberate a process; we see a greater spontaneity, that of the natural story-teller.

It is undoubtedly true that a great story can lose all its drama if the narrator is poorly equipped to tell it. The ability to tell a story bears little relation to academic attainment and training; some natural gift is necessary as well. Whatever that gift is, Mark possessed it. But a good story-teller also needs a good story if he is to make anything of it. In the Second Gospel story and story-teller are well-matched. For this reason Alex McCowen and others have been able to make a theatre success out of a solo reading of the book.

The dramatic element in Mark's composition appears in the continual alteration between the emphasis on the success of Jesus and his unpopularity, in the early hints of the final outcome and the stress on its inevitability, in the way the action is hurried forward from incident to incident through the first half of the Gospel by the use of 'immediately', in the heightening of tension as the opposition discloses itself fully first outside Jerusalem and then within the city, in the continual refusal of the group around Jesus to understand what he is about, in the falling away of that same group as the pressure increases, in the way in which the nature of discipleship is

---

[283] *Literary Criticism for New Testament Critics*, p. 58.

worked out through the construction of a journey by Jesus to his death in Jerusalem, in his silence as he is questioned by his judges, in his final loneliness on the cross and in the news that he has escaped the grave and would live again at the head of his followers.

The details of the individual pericopae show the same eye for the vivid phrase and the dramatic mood; often these have been regarded as a guarantee of the reliability of the tradition; more probably Mark himself has created them or stressed them in the already existing events in order to draw out the latent drama. Jesus stretches out his hand in compassion to touch a victim of the dreaded leprosy (1.41), the disciples testify that the winds and sea obey him (4.41), a woman goes to doctors who take her money and do her no good (5.26), Herod is trapped by a hasty promise and forced into executing John the Baptist (6.17–29), the Syro-Phoenician woman argues with Jesus and gains her point (7.24–30), the rich man departs droopingly (10.22), Peter breaks down and weeps after his denial (14.72).

The same dramatic element appears from another angle in the way Mark joins incidents together. Using his sandwich technique he inserts one within another so that the cleansing of the temple is illuminated by the cursing of the fig-tree; Israel has failed to bear the fruit for which God called and so is cursed (11.12–21). Peter's denial of his Lord comes between the affirmations by Jesus of his nature (14.61f.; 15.2). By the way incidents are placed in succession Mark brings out their drama; he moves Jesus directly from a discussion about the purity of Jewish life and customs (7.1–23) to the healing of a Gentile (7.24–30); the poor widow is commended for giving her all to a temple (12.41–44) whose destruction is already sealed (13.1–2); the prediction by Jesus of his death (8.31) is followed by a call to take up the cross and follow him (8.34); another prediction of the cross is succeeded by a picture of the disciples in their failure to understand arguing about their own relative greatness (9.30–34). Mark begins dramatically with Jesus appearing suddenly on the scene without father or mother or any earthly background. He also builds up to a climax: in the passion the crowds who welcomed him to Jerusalem disappear; the rulers of his own people bring him to trial; his disciples run away and leave him alone; the women look on from afar; he is completely isolated, even and above all from God, 'My God, my God why have you left me?' (15.34).

It is perhaps in the passion that the drama reaches its greatest intensity. Jesus speaks only three times, the cry of dereliction (15.34), the climax of his loneliness already seen in Gethsemane, and the two affirmations of his nature when challenged by the High

Priest and by Pilate (14.61f.; 15.2); otherwise he is silent (14.60; 15.4f.). But in what he says he has provided the crucial testimony for his condemnation. Here too in the Passion he is the king – crowned with thorns; the prophet – blindfolded and forced to prophesy who is striking him (15.17–20; 14.65). Here the false witnesses say what is true, that he will build a new temple not made with hands (14.58), and those who mock him on the cross enunciate the central soteriological paradox, 'He saved others; he cannot save himself' (15.31). In the end those who sought to kill him become themselves the tools of God in the accomplishment of salvation, for it is necessary that he should suffer and die (8.34). And through it all there is a certain dramatic irony; the readers know how it will finish; they can pick up the early references in 2.20 and 3.6; they know that the adulation of the crowd at the entry into Jerusalem will change to shouts of 'crucify him'.

Finally it is from the point of view of drama that we can appreciate most easily the conclusion to the Gospel. By its very nature the conclusion forces us to think out for ourselves the Gospel's challenge.[284] It would have been easy to finish with Jesus' victorious appearances to comfort the disciples: they all lived happily ever after. Instead the end is difficult: the women receive a message; they do not deliver it, for they are afraid. But if they never delivered it no one would ever have known about it, but Mark does and we do; therefore it was passed on. The women were afraid, and who would not be if they were told that someone was alive whom they had seen die before their eyes, and Mark makes sure to tell us that they saw him die and that they handled the corpse (15.40–47). Their fear is no more surprising than that of the disciples when Jesus walks to them on the sea while they labour at their rowing (6.45–52). The readers or hearers of Mark know the disciples did see Jesus; they also know that they themselves experience his powerful presence when they heal, preach and are persecuted. Where then is he? In Galilee at their head. What does that mean? Listen to the story as a believer and work it out for yourself. It is like one of Jesus' own parables: the hearer is forced to go on thinking.[285] Mark gives a clue to the way our minds should go in the word 'Galilee'. At the end we are taken back to the beginning: in 16.7 Jesus returns to Galilee whence he came in 1.9. Note similarly how the centurion's confession of Jesus as son of God (15.39) takes us back to God's confession of him as son at his baptism

[284] See above pp. 73–8.

[285] Cf. J. R. Donahue, 'Jesus as The Parable of God in the Gospel of Mark', *Int* 32 (1978) 369–386.

(1.11). There is no resting place in the joy and triumph of the resurrection; we have always to return to the beginning in Galilee and advance forward again to the cross. It is a continual pilgrimage, and the Christ whom we follow is both the crucified and the risen Christ. In that way the story is rounded off and we realise its unity.

CHAPTER XX

JESUS, PAST AND PRESENT

(8) Some of what we have written might suggest that Mark had no interest in the past. In relating Jesus to the present needs of the community does he not so contemporarize him as model of present behaviour to be followed and as present saviour and the disciples as displaying types of behaviour to be avoided that all interest in the Jesus of history disappears? Is the past of Jesus as past no longer of importance in itself? In contrast to Paul who is equally concerned about the present needs of the community Mark has chosen a narrative form in which the words and deeds of Jesus are the main feature. In contrast to John who allows for a continual contemporarization of Jesus with his doctrine of a Spirit who leads the church into truth Mark hardly speaks at all of the contemporary work of the Spirit in the church. The choice of a narrative form does not however of itself guarantee an interest in the past; almost all fiction has narrative form. In Mark's case however the narrative form chosen approximates to that of the biography. But the fictional biography is also a known literary form. Is there anything in Mark which would suggest he does not believe he is writing fictional biography? We have observed that he often refrains from adapting tradition to make it fit exactly into what appears to be his contemporary purpose. It is unimportant for the moment to ask after the accuracy of the tradition; what is important is Mark's attitude to it. He respects what has come to him from the past. He does not create incidents or sayings of Jesus to relate Jesus to the present need of his own community; his Jesus has nothing to say about spiritual gifts, about pagan worship (this hardly existed in Palestine but was the major religious feature of any Gentile community away from a Jewish controlled area), about the administration of the church and respect for its leaders. He does not present Jesus, as we might say, in Roman costume; he allows his 'foreignness' to remain; he is introduced at the very beginning as Jesus from Nazareth in Galilee (1.9). Aramaic words may be translated but major Jewish terms like 'Kingdom of God' and 'Christ' are unchanged. Between the sending out of the disciples (6.6b–13) and their return (6.30) nothing is recorded about Jesus; Mark inserts here his account of the death of John the Baptizer; he thus shows himself aware that events require reporters if they are to be

recorded; for a historical narrative witnesses are necessary. By setting Jesus' predictions of his death and resurrection and his instruction on discipleship within the framework of a journey with a named sequence of places visited he anchors both, and therefore Jesus himself, in past history. He takes care to show how trouble arose between Jesus and the Jews, particularly their leaders, as if he was seeking to trace the historical causes for Jesus' death (3.6; 11.27–33; 12.13; 14.1f.).[286] He preserves reminiscences of the disciples which do not show them at their best.

It might however be well asked whether Mark needed to guard against the danger of appearing to care little for the historical Jesus. Would anyone in his community ever have been worried by such fears? If it was the community in Rome then Peter, whom many of them would remember in their midst, was a firm guarantee to them of the historical Jesus as a figure of the recent past. The same would apply to any Christian community; they could easily trace the way back to the historical Jesus through the historical figures who in the beginning had brought them their knowledge of him. The stories Mark used must have come from somewhere and from some particular people.

There are other ways in which whether deliberately or unconsciously Mark shows the pastness of Jesus. Jesus appears on the scene 'in those days' (1.8) and 'those days' are the days of John the Baptizer. The readers know that John is dead so Jesus must belong to the past. In the framework of the story he mentions figures of the past, e.g. Pilate, and, more importantly, Peter whom his readers have themselves known and whom they now know to be dead. Mark's hearers would have no difficulty in accepting the pastness of Jesus.

But why does Mark emphasise Jesus' pastness? Jesus cannot be the risen saviour who still cares for the community unless he has first died. Moreover Mark connects the salvation of his community to the death of Jesus: he gave his life a ransom for them (10.45). Through his death the new people of God which is also the new temple replaces the old people (11.12–21; 14.58; 15.29; the latter two sayings are clearly true even if spoken by false witnesses or opponents). The heir to the vineyard is killed and so the vineyard is given to new tenants, the Christians (12.1–12). If Jesus had not died there would have been no salvation. Only if he belongs to the past can Jesus save his people.

Both the death and resurrection of Jesus are thus important for

[286] Cf. J. Roloff, 'Das Markusevangelium als Geschichtsdarstellung' in *Das Markus-Evangelium* (ed. R. Pesch), Darmstadt, 1979, pp. 283–310 = *Ev.Th.* 29 (1969) 73–93.

Mark. His death ensures that he belongs to the past and is saviour through the effects of that death. His resurrection ensures that he is still with his community to shepherd and care for it. But his life with its activity and teaching must equally have been important or Mark would not have spent so much of his book recounting it. His mighty deeds and words cannot then be dismissed as merely preliminary details for a passion narrative.[287]

We have seen that Bultmann held the origin of the Gospel to lie in the marriage of the hellenistic kerygma and the tradition about Jesus. If the hellenistic kerygma is that of a descending and ascending saviour then there is little or no trace of that in Mark's Gospel. Jesus appears on the scene at his baptism by John without any reference to a previous heavenly existence. At the end he is said to have risen, not to have ascended; if Mark had wished to depict Jesus as a hellenistic saviour he only needed to make the message to the women at the tomb one about his ascension.[288] The kerygma of a descending and ascending saviour was not the only kerygma in use in the early church. There is probably one concealed in 1 Th 1.9f. where the Christian is described as one who has turned from idols to serve the living and true God and who awaits his son Jesus from heaven, whom God raised from the dead and who delivers from the wrath to come. With its reference to Jesus this kerygma acknowledges in some way his earthly life and like Mark characterises him as 'son'. But Mark refers much more to his earthly life, brings in his death and does not stress the wrath to come. The narrative element which we have seen to form so large a part of Mark's Gospel is thus missing. There is a sense in which this was present in the hellenistic kerygma, only the narrative is set in the heavenly world rather than in the earthly. The element of earthly narrative begins to appear in the kerygma of 1 Cor 15.3–5, 'died, buried, raised, appeared' but it commences too far into the life of Jesus to have been a model for Mark. The post-Markan summary of the gospel in Acts 10.36–43 gives a brief account of Jesus' earthly life before it refers to his death. It does not relate redemption to the death of Jesus (contrast 1 Cor 15.3) as Mark does but includes it as one item in a list of events. In a sense Mark's kerygma is a mixture of the narratives of Acts 10.36–43[289] and 1 Cor 15.3–5, though naturally it would be wrong to think of it as a deliberate unification of the two. Since only the latter pre-dates Mark it is better to contrast Mark with it than with the former. Like Mark

[287] As Kähler (see n. 104), p. 80, n. 11, appears to do.
[288] For this view and criticism see above pp. 76–8 and n. 158.
[289] It is assumed that we do not have Peter's original speech here in Acts 10.

1 Cor 15.3–5 lacks any idea of the pre-existence of Jesus; it also, unlike Mark, lacks any account of the events of Jesus' earthly life prior to his death. Mark then has introduced here a new element: the earthly life of Jesus. He has also dropped the final item 'He appeared to Cephas, then to the twelve'. It is not as we have seen[290] that he disbelieves that Jesus appeared to Peter and the twelve. The omission must be deliberate (assuming the Gospel ended at 16.8). He has no resurrection appearances because Christ is present throughout the whole Gospel as the one who cares. The extent and manner of his present caring is known through the way he once cared. It is from what Jesus once was that Mark knows what he now is and this explains why he repeats the tradition of Jesus' earthly activity. There is continuity between the life of the church and the life of Jesus. That is not to say that the church continues the incarnation, for much of what Jesus did the church cannot do: he alone redeems. But in some of the other ways in which he ministered to men it continues and repeats his work. What it does, it does however not in its own strength but in his, or in the strength on which he taught it to draw, that of God experienced through prayer or the Spirit. On the other hand for Mark there was no possibility as there was for the Fourth Evangelist that more teaching and new types of activity would come from the exalted Jesus through the witness of the Spirit. Mark does not consciously extend the sayings or actions of Jesus beyond what he has received in the tradition. The original teaching and activity will live again and are not to be supplanted or supplemented.

Even if we were to suppose that Mark had set out to unite the kerygma and the Jesus-tradition we can now see that what he has in fact done is much more. He has set each item of the tradition in relation to other items and so shed new light on their significance. As for the kerygma it has undergone profound modification in its union with the tradition. After what Mark has done neither Jesus-tradition nor kerygma can ever be the same again. The kerygma possesses a new and important element and the question of the historical Jesus can no longer be evaded, though by the very way in which the kerygma has been married to the traditions about Jesus it is difficult to answer questions about what actually happened.

We have tried to identify Mark's kerygma, as earlier we attempted to give a brief summary of the Gospel. It may be that both these attempts contradict Mark's actual intention since they lift attention from both the detail of the narrative and the fact that it is narrative.

---

[290] Pp. 72–4.

It may well be that this is what Mark specifically wished to avoid. It is only as we read what he wrote as a whole and not in summary that it can make its impact.

Sometimes the ransom saying (10.45) is isolated from its context and learned discussions take place as to whom the ransom is paid; a transaction theology results. For Mark the saying is the climax of his discussion of the general ministering activity of Jesus; it sums up what precedes and illuminates the death that follows. The death of Jesus is only to be understood in the light of his life. This is very different from the interpretation of Hebrews which sets it against the background of the Jewish sacrificial system.

Earlier we saw that the geographical outline with the contrast of Galilee and Jerusalem was deliberately shaped by Mark. This outline possesses a theological motif. It forces us to attend to the kind of person Jesus was and is before it recounts his death and resurrection. The death and resurrection is not some isolated event which could soon lose its place in history and become purely mythological. It is the death and resurrection of someone who called particular disciples, healed particular people, told particular parables, challenged men to follow him in a particular way.

Discipleship itself can only be seen in the light of the total story of Jesus. It is not a question of obedience to a set of commandments or of continual aspiration after an ideal. The narrative provides examples and links them together so that it is seen to be a life-long following of Jesus as he ministers to others and goes the way of the cross; failures in following are vividly illustrated in the behaviour of the disciples. Readers know the disciples did not finally apostatise and so they realise that they themselves will never be reduced as Jesus was to crying 'My God, my God, why have you abandoned me?'

If the soteriology lies not in individual statements like the ransom saying but in the whole narrative this is equally true of the christology. There are certainly formal statements: Jesus is son of God and son of man. But the narrative provides a wider canvas. What theologians term the true manhood of Jesus appears clearly in what he suffers, especially in the passive suffering of the cross. There is no divine intervention; Elijah does not come as the cry of dereliction leads some to suppose he will; the prayer of Gethsemane 'Let this cup pass' is not granted. But the other side of the story is also brought out. Jesus sets down in prophecy a way to go (8.31, etc.) and he goes that way without failure. By contrast the disciples who are challenged to go fail, for they are wholly human. He forgives sins (2.10), which is God's privilege alone. He calls the temple, which is God's house, 'my house' (11.17). He sets aside current interpretation of the law and proclaims his authority over it (2.28; 7.1–23). In these and other ways the divine side of his being is set forth.

Mark sees the historical Jesus and the preached Christ as one and the same; therefore he retells the events of the earthly life of Jesus at the same time as he presents him through these as son of God and son of man. The gospel which Jesus is said to proclaim is given in 1.14f. in a mixture of Jesus' own terms (e.g. kingdom of God) and those of the early church (e.g. believe, gospel). That Jesus is said to 'speak the word' (8.32; 2.2; 4.33)[291] links what he did to what Christian missionaries do, for the early Christians used the phrase of preaching the gospel (e.g. Acts 4.29,31; 8.25). In 8.32 Jesus speaks plainly of his death and resurrection and this is to proclaim what is central to the gospel. At 2.2 where Mark again says Jesus 'speaks the word', he offers the forgiveness of sins (2.3–12). He teaches with authority (1.21f.) and that authority is power over the demonic world (1.23–26); he gives the same power to his followers (3.15). The result of Jesus' teaching is set out in 4.14–20 and this is expressed in the terms of the experience of the church (note the use of 'speak the word' in 4.33). The well-known ambiguity of the genitive in 'the gospel of Jesus Christ' in the opening words of the book is probably to be understood in the same way: he is at once the proclaimer and the proclaimed. What the one who goes to the cross preaches is the same as what is preached through the church by the risen Christ. So when we hear the words of the historical Jesus and read of his deeds we encounter the words and deeds of the risen and preached Christ.

[291] On 'the word' in Mark see Best, as n. 103, pp. 70f.

CHAPTER XXI

A GOSPEL GENRE?

(9) There have been as we have seen various attempts to characterise the book that Mark wrote. In the second half of the nineteenth century it was regarded as history. More recently it has been taken as apocalyptic literature (H.C. Kee), as biography (Stanton, Talbert), as apology (Moule), as sermon (Marxsen), as drama (Standaert). It has been described as a passion narrative with extended introduction[292] but the so-called introduction is not an introduction but an inherent part of the book and must be accorded much greater importance than Kähler gave it. Dibelius called it a book of secret epiphanies[293] but this does not take sufficient account of the importance of the passion. None of these characterisations are adequate in and of themselves as descriptions of the book.

Is it a new type of writing? Have we here a new genre? This is a tempting solution. If Christianity is unique may not its foundation documents be also? Yet Paul used the existing literary form of the letter. There may be no letter in the ancient world to which his letters are precisely similar but in the ancient world there was a great variety of forms of letters and no single rigid form. Paul's letters do not follow any one of these forms yet clearly what he wrote can be described as 'letter'. There is then no need for Christianity to be expressed in utterly new literary forms. The theory that the gospel is a new genre (the idea appears to go back to Franz Overbeck[294]) has even been extended to the view that Mark belongs to a different genre from the other gospels.[295] Clearly the Gospel of Thomas and the Gospel of Truth together with Q (if it existed) are different in form from the four canonical gospels in that they have little in the way of narrative and what they have does not create a continuous story. They belong to a different genre. The four canonical gospels however are sufficiently similar to be regarded as belonging to the same genre. But are they a new genre? As Petersen points out, if a gospel was an absolutely new

[292] Kähler, as n. 104, p. 80, n. 11.
[293] As n. 239, p. 230.
[294] So Güttgemanns, as n. 10, p. 158.
[295] Cf. S. Schulz, 'Die Bedeutung des Markus für die Theologiegeschichte des Urchristentums' in R. Pesch, as n. 286, pp. 151–162 at p. 151 = *TU* 87, pp. 135–145.

genre there would be a difficulty in communication. 'New genres certainly emerge but they must do so differentially in relation to other genres in a generic system'.[296] At the same time, however, we must remember, as Wilder has emphasised,[297] that form and content are related. If there is a difference between Christianity and other faiths, and all faiths and philosophies are different from one another, the form of the communication of Christianity will differ in some ways from the forms of communication of other religions and philosophies. But since Christianity lies nearer to Judaism than to any other faith we should not be surprised if the Gospel genre lies near to Jewish writing.

Mark has similarities with a number of other kinds of writings. It is narrative though the narrative is not put forward as fiction. It is consequently closer to biography. Unlike biography it is concerned to advance an ideological position and move its readers to practise more zealously the faith to which they are committed. In that respect it is more like a sermon. Narrative with the intention of influencing people to new behaviour is of course not an entirely unknown genre. *Gulliver's Travels, Uncle Tom's Cabin, Nineteen Eighty Four* are examples, though in each case the narrative is fiction. Ancient biography was often used to present ideal behaviour and history was written so that lessons could be drawn. In neither case however was theology involved. Perhaps then the nearest parallel to the gospel genre is to be found within Judaism, firstly in the Old Testament and then in later books like those of the Maccabees. The Deuteronomic historian was a profound theologian.

Such a view is reinforced when we remember that the literature with which Mark was likely to be best acquainted was neither the histories and biographies of the Greeks and Romans nor the works of their rhetoricians and dramatists of none of which does he show any awareness but the Old Testament.

> Hebrew thinking is thinking in historical traditions; that is, its main concern is with the proper combination of traditions and their theological interpretation, and in the process historical grouping always takes precedence over intellectual and theological grouping.[298]

There are of course different types of historical narrative in the Old

---

[296] Op. cit., p. 44; cf. F. Kermode, *The Genesis of Secrecy: On the Interpretation of Narrative,* London, 1979, pp. 162f., n. 20.

[297] As n. 229, pp. 33ff.

[298] G. von Rad, *Old Testament Theology* (ET by D.M.G. Stalker) Vol I, Edinburgh, 1962, p. 116.

Testament. We can distinguish on the one hand between the myths of the early chapters of Genesis and the parabolic stories of Ruth and Jonah in which there is no real basis in fact and on the other hand the narratives in the historical books where there is some substratum of actual events. Mark would probably have made no such distinction in respect of the Old Testament but would have regarded all the narratives as founded on fact. Within the Old Testament he would find the series of stories about Abraham, Joseph, Saul, David which he would accept as true. Why should he himself not compose something similar? Naturally its content would be different because Jesus differed from Abraham, Joseph, Saul, David, just as they differed from each other. Incidentally the re-editing of Mark by Matthew and Luke to some extent resembles the way the Old Testament traditions were re-worked from period to period. In his re-writing of Mark Luke clearly shows that unlike Mark he was influenced by contemporary literature and the way it was written. The matrix of Mark's Gospel however is the Old Testament.[299]

Confirmation of this may be seen in the way Mark's narrative style corresponds to that of the narrative portions of the Old Testament. J. Licht isolates four modes of narrative: straight narrative, scenic narrative, description, comment. 'In straight narrative the author simply reports a series of events, telling his audience that this and this happened . . . In scenic narrative, by contrast, the action is broken up into a sequence of scenes . . . Conflicts, direct statements of single acts, and direct speech are pre-eminent.' In description 'the storyteller stops the flow of events, taking his time to tell the audience how persons, places and objects looked or sounded or smelled . . . comment comprises remark which explain the situation, praise or blame the characters, point the moral and generally help the story along.'[300] Licht concludes that 'the narrative mode of the Hebrew Bible is predominantly scenic'.[301] In Mark we have some straight narrative, e.g. the steps of the journey from Caesarea Philippi to Jerusalem, but it is a minor element.[302] There is almost no description; Jesus is never described and the description of John the Baptizer is theologically motivated to present him as Elijah. Comment does not occupy a large part of the Gospel; the hardness of heart and fear of the disciples are only brief comments like those passed in the Old

---

[299] Compare the quotation from Sanders given on p. 127.

[300] J. Licht, *Storytelling in the Bible*, Jerusalem, 1978, pp. 29f.

[301] Ibid. p. 50.

[302] Cf. R. Alter, *The Art of Biblical Narrative*, London, 1981, pp. 65f.

Testament on various judges and kings; sometimes there is comment on Jesus, often in words drawn from the Old Testament (contrast the comments in Paul's speech at Athens which are drawn from secular literature). By far the largest part of the narrative of the Gospel is 'scenic'. Too much cannot be made of this since it may be a natural result of using narrative oral material which might itself tend to be 'scenic'. However it shows the Gospel as lying much closer to the Old Testament than to much contemporary Greek literature. Another factor indicating the influence of the Old Testament on Mark is the prevalence of direct speech over indirect.[303]

The form critics have taught us to see a particular form associated with a particular *Sitz im Leben*. The more we regard the Gospel as a unique genre the more difficult this becomes; it is impossible to generalise from four examples. If however the genre bears some resemblance to sections of the Old Testament this would suggest that we look for its association with a setting in which there is respect for leaders in religion from the past, leaders whose lives as well as their teaching would be of importance to their followers. Writings like Q, the Gospel of Thomas, the Quran of course would appear where the teaching alone is taken as all-important. However even in Mark's time the Jewish religious community was still producing literature in which past events in the lives of particular people were retold because of their importance for the present, e.g. The Book of Jubilees, the Biblical Antiquities of Pseudo-Philo, the Antiquities of Josephus. The Gospels fit into this kind of situation.

Most of this literature however appeared long after the events with which it deals, but this is true only of the final forms which we now possess. Pseudo-Philo and Josephus are dependent on earlier material; so is the biblical material as we now have it. We cannot say how soon after the death of Joseph, Moses, Abraham or David the cycles of stories about them were formed out of the earlier individual stories. It probably took some time. It also took some time before the Gospel of Mark appeared. This may help us to see why it took forty years and not ten from Jesus' death. Today biographies of famous men and women appear not only at their death but even during their lifetime. Jesus' life was too short for the latter, but why did Mark or someone else not write sooner? Unlike today there was no group of readers ready to seize on the latest biography, push up its sales and reward writer and publisher. The

---

[303] Ibid., pp. 67ff.

only interested people would be the Christians and there were not many of them. Moreover they already knew the stories as individual accounts or in collections of related accounts. What led to the appearance of the Gospel from these we have discussed earlier in relation to its occasion; it was not sociological pressure leading to the marriage of the kerygma and Jesus tradition but a need of the community and we have viewed this as a failure to appreciate the sacrifice required from the members if they were to be true followers of their Lord rather than as their need to fight off some heresy gaining ground among them.

As well as discussing the *Sitz im Leben* of the Gospel genre, whether unique or not, we must say something of the life of the actual community out of which Mark appeared. While it may seem trite it is important to emphasise that it was a Christian community. After that beginning we have to be very cautious in anything we may say because of the very nature of the writing as one which uses tradition and considers the past of its main figure as important. We have seen that Mark preserves the tradition in the form the community knew it; we cannot know to what extent the community had previously modified it or, more importantly, gradually forgotten stories which had no relevance to its own life. We can only work from what has been preserved. If it has been preserved it must not be assumed that every detail was relevant to the lives of its readers. If parables of Jesus are used which depend on rural imagery this does not mean that the community is rural. If warnings are given against riches (10.17ff.) this does not mean that the community consisted of rich men and women; it will probably have had some wealthy members. More importantly, the community has probably lasted long enough for the first flush of enthusiasm to have been lost. It was in danger of slipping back into 'the easy and self-indulgent life which seemed to be the goal of the Graeco-Roman world'[304] Mark knew. There is an unwillingness to go the way of the cross. The temptations outlined in 4.14–20 are probably real. The community knows about persecution; how much it has suffered is not clear; everything indicates that it fears further persecution for Mark has given prominence to the call to take up the cross. It has been very interested in apocalypticism and Mark attempts to quieten this interest (13.32), though he does not in any way seek to eliminate the parousia and stress a thoroughly realised eschatology. Although there is no idea of its members as wandering charismatic preachers, assuming that is what Jesus desired his first

[304] P.J. Achtemeier, 'Mark as Interpreter of the Jesus Traditions', *Int* 32 (1978) 339–352.

followers to be, the members are not exercising the gift of healing and need to relearn how the sick are to be healed (9.28f.). Only a few are expected to go off as missionaries; the call to give up their possessions is not laid on all. By and large they had forgotten that Jesus could care for all their spiritual needs; they found his death difficult to understand; they could not see the need for suffering on their own part; there was a slackening of their realisation of the radical nature of the Christian way of life which they had adopted.

There was probably no large block of Jewish converts among them; although there is material which reflects controversy about the Jewish law there is not an excessive amount of it; the tradition was bound to contain some. Its absence does not mean that they were free of contact with Jews. The controversy about the admission of Gentiles appears to be over for there is little about it and it is assumed that Gentiles are in the church. If there is polemic from the Gentile angle it is polemic not against Jewish Christians but against Jews as such, for Mark emphasises the existence of Christians as the people of God in place of the Jews. The temple has been cleansed and Judaism has lost its place; the rending of the veil of the temple, the parable of the tenants in the vineyard with its interpretation (12.1–12), the clear rejection of Jesus by the Jewish nation and people all indicate the same. Christians had suffered persecution from Jews in the first days of the church; there is no hint that they are likely to suffer again from Jews; but the Jews have a privileged place in the Empire. If Christians cannot claim to have this position and be well-treated by the Roman authorities, let them at least remember that now they have a superior position to the Jews before God.

How else was the Gospel to be used in the life of the church? It was certainly not written as a book for dissection in the study or as an aid to private devotion. If on the other hand it was to be used publicly it was not to be divided up into fragments like a lectionary. If its impact was to be in public and if its full impact can only be perceived when it is read or heard as a whole, when would a book be put into use whose public reading would occupy two hours? To us this seems an enormously long time. We should not judge by our standards. It is not so long since the preacher whose sermons did not last at least an hour was regarded in Protestant circles as a failure. The Gospel of Mark is only half as long again as 1 Corinthians and Paul expected his letters to be read aloud in church. The reading of the Gospel might then have been the special feature of some services. Its long treatment of the passion suggests a service centred on this, making Easter a strong possibility, but we can go no further than that with even a measure of probability.

CHAPTER XXII

THE GOSPEL'S CONTINUING SIGNIFICANCE

Mark was writing for a particular situation in a particular place at a particular time. What then is the value of his book for us who live at a different time and in very different situations? His generation believed in personal forces of evil as possessing men; we do not; we may believe in them 'officially' but we do not reckon with them in our day-to-day life. His generation had no difficulty in accepting that five loaves and two fish were sufficient to feed five thousand people; ours has. We do not think easily of a contest between God and the power of evil. The concept of Jesus as bearing the judgement of God seems immoral to some; why should men not bear their own judgement? If we live in a community with Jews do we want to emphasise God's replacement of them by us as his people; if not what is the relevance of the rejection of Israel? Yet on the other hand we may value Mark for a reason for which it was probably not written: as a mine of historical information about Jesus. If Mark and the other Gospels had not appeared would Christianity have survived? Paul can easily be read in such a way that Jesus becomes a cipher, a mythical figure who dies and rises like many of the central figures in the mystery religions. Certainly the nineteenth century put too great an emphasis on Jesus as a figure in history and assumed that through our knowledge of that figure men could be saved. The reaction of the dialectical theology of Barth and Bultmann was a necessary reaction but it in itself required a correction lest Jesus again began to become only a cipher. Today then there is a new quest for the historical Jesus. Those who take part in it certainly realise that the search is itself much more difficult than it appeared in the nineteenth century but they believe it is a search which must be carried on. If the mind of Jesus is to be in us then we must know something of that mind. We must also know that there is some measure of continuity between Jesus and the gospel which was preached about him. If we did not have Mark and the Gospels which followed him we would not even be able to begin to consider these questions.

However all that is a by-product of our possession of Mark's Gospel. More directly in line with his purpose in writing is the view of discipleship which he sets out. Mark did not expect that it would be long until the return of Jesus and the end of the journey on which he and his fellow Christians had entered would be reached. He was wrong. Yet the way in which he presented the journey is capable of indefinite extension; it is in no way linked to the return of Jesus, for it is set in terms of the cross and the resurrection. The basic teaching which Mark gives about the nature of greatness and the need to lose oneself remains as true now as it was then, and as necessary. His radical discussion of discipleship plumbs the very depths of the nature of Christianity. We are as unwilling to accept it as Mark's community was. But Mark also saw that in order to go the way of a disciple it was not sufficient to imitate Jesus; imitation was impossible without the help of Jesus himself. Thus he gives a central place to Jesus; it is from Jesus that discipleship begins; it is because of Jesus and what he has done that discipleship is possible. So Mark in his central drive can still mediate to us an understanding of Christian faith.

ABBREVIATIONS

Bib	Biblica.
CBQ	Catholic Biblical Quarterly.
ET	English Translation.
ETL	Ephemerides Theologicae Lovanienses.
EvTh	Evangelische Theologie.
Int	Interpretation.
JBL	Journal of Biblical Literature.
JSNT	Journal for the Study of the New Testament.
JTS	Journal of Theological Studies.
NT	Novum Testamentum.
NTS	New Testament Studies.
RB	Revue Biblique.
SBT	Studies in Biblical Theology.
SE	Studia Evangelica.
TU	Texte und Untersuchungen.

INDEX OF AUTHORS

INDEX OF PASSAGES CITED